CW00455437

"The Bottom Shop"
The History of Glassmaking in Hatton, Derbyshire

Chris Tipper and Philip Bell

© Christopher S Tipper and Philip A Bell 2022

All Rights Reserved. No part of this publication may be reproduced, stored in a retrieval system, or transmitted in any form, or by any means, electronic, mechanical, photocopying, recording or otherwise without the prior permission in writing of the copyright holders.

British Library Cataloguing in Publication Data.

A catalogue record for this book is available from the British Library

ISBN 978 0 86071 888 8

For further information regarding this book, please contact:
Tutbury Museum
Charity House, Duke Street, Tutbury, Staffordshire DE139NE
Website: www.tutburymuseum.org   Email: tutburymuseum@gmail.com

A Commissioned Publication Printed by

MOORLEYS
Print, Design & Publishing
info@moorleys.co.uk • www.moorleys.co.uk

This story of Hatton Glassworks has been written as part of a project for Tutbury Museum on the history of glassmaking in the local area. The book is published with the aim of bringing new research evidence to the knowledge of a wider public and of illustrating the Museum's local history resources.

The book is dedicated to the memory of our fathers, Stuart Tipper and Wilfred James Bell, both life-long Glass Cutters, and to our many extended family members for whom the Hatton and Tutbury Glassworks provided the background to their lives.

Contents

1.   Introduction

A little geographical clarification may be helpful first. Today's bustling centre of Hatton village, located close to the railway crossing, is a relatively modern creation. In the early nineteenth century, before the coming of the railway, Hatton was a scattered, largely agricultural settlement. The name "Hatton" appears generally to have been used more in reference to the farms and cottages towards and beyond the Derby to Uttoxeter turnpike road, past today's "Salt Box" junction. The land bounded by the Scropton Old and New Lanes and Marston Old and New Lanes had little identity of its own. Despite being in Derbyshire, this area immediately north of the River Dove was treated for many official purposes as part of the long-established village of Tutbury on the southern bank of the river in Staffordshire.

The original naming of the railway station situated in its midst as Tutbury Station was the most enduring manifestation of this. Hatton had no church of its own till the late 1800's, and its inhabitants had to make their way to Marston, Scropton or Tutbury churches for their baptisms, marriages and burials. Its postal facilities came under the umbrella of Tutbury, which had the local mail sorting office and later the telephone exchange. In 19th century Trade Directories, Hatton businesses usually appear only in Staffordshire editions, within the Tutbury section.

The Hatton glassworks, in its various guises, was therefore frequently referred to by outsiders as "Tutbury Glassworks" and in many sources is not distinguished from and is often confused with the pre-existing glassmaking factory in Ludgate Street, Tutbury.   But for local residents, there was never any confusion about the two glassworks: up in Ludgate Street was "the Top Shop"; down by the river in Hatton was "the Bottom Shop".

Glassmaking in Hatton took place on one site in Scropton Lane, bounded by the North Staffordshire Railway line. The operation traded first as William Alexander Sivewright & Son; then as the Royal Castle Glass Works ("RCGW"), under the proprietorship firstly of JTH Richardson & Sons and later of Corbett & Co Ltd; then as British Thomson-Houston Co Ltd and Webbs Crystal Glass Co Ltd; and finally as Trent Valley Glassworks ("TVGW"). There was also a short-lived venture on an adjoining plot, the Anchor & Cross Bottle Works.

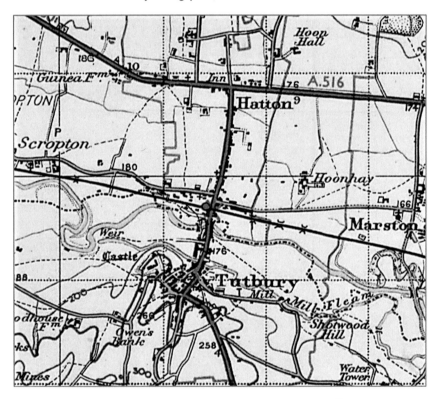

Figure 1 - Hatton and Tutbury in the Early 20th Century

Ordnance Survey New Popular Edition One-Inch Map, Sheet 120. Full revision 1917, with later corrections to 1947, but generally indicative of the locality in the first part of the 20th century.

2

On this blow-up of the previous map the Scropton Lane Industrial site is the narrow rectangular area immediately west of the station (red dot), bordered on the south by the railway line and on the north by New Scropton Lane (yellow). It ran from west of the Methodist Chapel, marked as a cross, towards the first gridline.

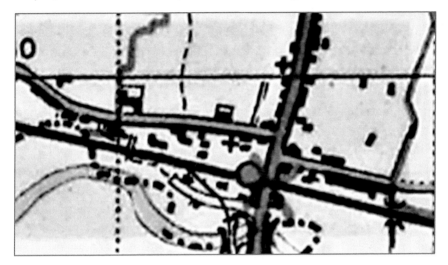

Figure 2 - Scropton Lane

Several separate structures are recorded in black within this area. The Royal Castle Glass Works is the most westerly of these. The building footprint roughly reflects the cover page 1879 image.

Old Scropton Lane is shown in white, running from between the station and river in a WNW direction - the original route from Tutbury to Scropton, it had been severed by the building of the railway in the 1840's and became disused except for foot traffic, replaced by the newly built New Scropton Lane.

The glassworks is the first industrial concern known to have appeared on the site. Other buildings on the site at different times housed the

Photo Decorated Tileworks, the Anchor & Cross Bottle Works, the Trades Progress Company, Tutbury Engineering, Record Engineering, and, latterly, Clayton Equipment.

No Tithe Apportionment Maps covering the Hatton area appear to exist, but the tithe maps for Tutbury (1841) and Scropton (1847) parishes, which closely border the site, indicate that the land bounding New Scropton Lane was purely agricultural at those times, and they show no evident commercial structures.

An outline of the history of glassmaking in Hatton has been known for some years. Much of this derived from the research of Mr WH Bennett during his time as Managing Director of TVGW. In particular, he established contact with former Scropton Lane workers Frank Pegg and Wilfred Woolley in their retirement in 1955 and 1973 respectively. Their recollections, together with other documents, provided material for the first section of a short 1984 paper, "The Hatton Glassmakers", produced by Mr Harry Shaw, General Manager at Trent Valley. This documentation was deposited with Tutbury Museum, along with several lengthy internal reports on key events during the period of TVGW's operation. These were supplemented by the text for a presentation prepared by local historian Aubrey Bailey, which pulled together what was then known about the era of the RCGW, as well as an extensive description of the operating departments in TVGW's time. Several informative sets of photographs have survived - these include group pictures of the workforce around the turn of the 20th century and photos of engraved glass from that time, donated by the Crossley family, together with others covering the Trent Valley era from former employees.

But all that was known of the very earliest period of operations in the 19th century could be told in just a few sentences. More recent research has enabled a much fuller picture to be painted, both of

4

Hatton's glassmaking enterprises and of a number of related neighbouring industrial operations. Among the resources that have contributed to this are:

- The Flint Glass Makers' Magazine, the quarterly journal of the glassblowers' trade union, the Flint Glass Makers' Friendly Society, of which an almost complete set for the period 1850 to 1903 is held by the Modern Records Centre of the University of Warwick;

- Companies House filings for Corbett & Co Ltd, and background information on the life of George Harry Corbett, made available by Mr Ron Dent, a descendant of Mr Corbett;

- Other Companies House filings for the Anchor & Cross Bottle Works Syndicate Ltd, the Photo Decorated Tile Company Ltd and the Trades Progress Company Ltd.

- National and regional newspaper reports, now accessible and searchable on-line from various sources, together with local Burton-on-Trent and Derby newspapers held by the Magic Attic in Swadlincote;

- Large scale Ordnance Survey maps of the Hatton area, for which valuable interpretation has been provided by Mr Tony Beresford;

- Standard family history research resources of censuses, parish registers of baptisms, marriages and burials, and civil registrations of births, marriages and deaths, accessed through transcriptions prepared by Robert and Jeanne Minchin of Tutbury Museum and through commercial family history databases;

- Commercial Trade Directories from the Victorian period;

- Personal recollections of Mr Harry Shaw, Mr Jack Mear and other former TVGW employees and local residents;

- Information from descendants of William Sivewright in New Zealand.

The Hatton Glassworks story that emerges is less cohesive, but arguably more eventful and colourful than that of Tutbury Glassworks, which had a 200-year continuity of operation (with only very brief interruptions in 1880 and 1980), and a substantial degree of consistency in the type of glass that it produced. Hatton's operations, by contrast, ran across a period of 120 years, during which time they were punctuated by three closures lasting a total of 37 years. The Hatton output also ranged from the sophistication of hand-blown and decorated crystal tableware to the more mundane machine-based production of cosmetic containers, jam jars, light bulbs and even dolls eyes.

The one element of continuity was the Scropton Lane site. The story is best told by looking in detail at the various enterprises that set up in business there, and by trying to bring back to life the very different entrepreneurs who ran them. They will be examined in chronological order, firstly in brief summary and then in detail.

The intention is that the tone will be that of a story, more of a "tale" than an academic history, as this seems best suited to the roller-coaster enterprise that was the Hatton Glassworks. There will no doubt be errors in this book, hopefully not too many of fact, but certainly of interpretation, for which the authors apologise in advance. Historical detective work is never complete and new information regularly comes to light, leading to frequent reassessment of aspects of the story. Any comments, corrections and additions are welcome.

Summary History of Glassmaking in Hatton

1863-1868   **William Alexander Sivewright & Son**

Glassmaking was first established on a site in Scropton Lane, Hatton by William A. Sivewright in partnership with his son. Sivewright had been employed as a Glass Blower at Jackson's Tutbury Glassworks for 25 years, and was a leading figure in the industry through his position as national Secretary of the Flint Glass Makers' Friendly Society. In 1863 he resigned from this Trade Union and "crossed sides" to set himself up as an employer, manufacturing decorated glass tableware in what was first called the "New Glassworks". He recruited a number of skilled fellow Tutbury craftsmen to join him, employing around forty people in total. The partnership went bankrupt in 1868 and production ceased. Some skilled staff were re-located around the country under a Union scheme, but many eventually found their way back to the Tutbury Glassworks.

1871-1900   **John Thomas Haden Richardson & Sons**

JTH Richardson was from a famous family of glass manufacturers in Stourbridge. He came to Tutbury in 1863 to manage the Jackson family's Glassworks. This he did energetically, patenting technical improvements in the glassblowing process. But in 1871 he left to set up on his own account on the Hatton site, manufacturing and decorating flint glass tableware. The business flourished and by the 1880's a substantial factory had developed in Scropton Lane. First known as the Castle Glassworks, it soon styled itself the "Royal Castle Glass Works". (Royalty did indeed turn up on the doorstep many years after.) In 1880 it was advertising itself "By Royal Letters Patent, Manufacturers of all kinds of Flint, Emerald & Ruby Glass, Cut & Engraved, for Home and Export Trade." He employed in excess of sixty workers. But after many vicissitudes during a long trade depression, the RCGW ceased manufacture at the turn of the century.

1905-1910   **The Anchor & Cross Bottle Works**

A group of London investors established a "model" factory for the automatic production of glass bottles in Scropton Lane in 1905. The factory was designed and built by the neighbouring engineers, The Trades Progress Company, led by Vincent J McIntyre. The promoters tried to capitalise on American advances in automation, making a virtue of unskilled labour at the expense of what they saw as outdated hand-blowing craft skills. A private railway siding ran into the works from Tutbury Station. Technical problems hampered the early years, most spectacularly in 1908 when a furnace collapsed and 32 tons of red-hot molten glass spread out across the factory floor. The company's suppliers and markets were mainly in the South East and rail freight costs made the business uncompetitive. In 1910 the plant was dismantled and moved by a special train, along with many employees, their families and worldly goods, to a new site in Kent.

1910-1920   **Corbett & Co and Webbs Crystal Glass**

George Harry Corbett was a born salesman, but over-ambition led him too far. In 1910 he left the management of Thomas Webb & Corbett's Tutbury factory, which he'd successfully run for four years, and reopened the derelict Royal Castle Glass Works, making lightly blown, cut and engraved lead glassware. Many of the best Tutbury blowers and decorators joined him, and they are pictured together in an evocative photo of an early works outing to Dovedale. By 1912 he was already in financial difficulties and Stanley Jenkinson of the well-known Edinburgh & Leith Flint Glass Company came in as an investor. Within a short while Corbett was acrimoniously forced out of his employment and controlling shareholding. The factory was substantially expanded in 1916/17, including the introduction of two modern Hermanson furnaces. In 1920 the Hatton operation was purchased and merged with several other glassmakers into a major new national group, Webb's Crystal Glass Company Ltd.

1914-1924   **British Thomson-Houston Co Ltd**

Before WW1 most electric light bulb production in Europe had been based in Germany and Austria. With the outbreak of hostilities, the UK authorities had to rapidly establish a viable home industry. This was directed through British Thomson-Houston Co Ltd of Rugby. Towards the end of 1914 BTH arranged with Jenkinson for the RCGW factory to use its lead glass for light bulb and tube production. The local blowers were unhappy with the sidelining of their craft skills, went on strike and were sacked. Their places were taken by specialist bulb blowers recruited from France. With demand increasing, BTH installed the semi-automatic "Empire Bulb-blowing Machine", aided by the electrification of the plant. The Glassworks ceased operations in 1924. It remained as a BTH store until 1928, but then lay empty till 1939 when it was requisitioned by the War Department for storage.

1946-1984   **Trent Valley Glassworks**

William Bennett of Glastics Ltd acquired the derelict Scropton Lane factory in 1946 and re-opened its glassmaking facilities in 1947, under his son, WH Bennett. The father's entrepreneurial acumen was not matched by his geographical precision and this operation by the River Dove was christened Trent Valley Glassworks. Processes were semi-automated, producing a range of moulded glassware, particularly for the perfume and cosmetics markets. Post-war shortages created early challenges, but production facilities were substantially upgraded over the following thirty years. At the height of its success, it employed around 200 people. The factory had its share of bad luck, with major flooding in 1957 and 1960 and fires in 1971 and 1977, from all of which it was able to quickly recover. The trading environment finally deteriorated, with competition from fully-automated producers with lower wage costs. The factory closed in 1984. The site was later developed for housing and no trace of its industrial past remains.

2.   1863-1868   William Alexander Sivewright & Son

William Alexander Sivewright is the forgotten hero of the glass industry in Hatton and Tutbury.

Born in Newcastle-upon-Tyne in 1811, Sivewright, a Glass Blower by trade, came to Tutbury in the late 1830's in response to Henry Jackson's recruitment drive after the expansion of his Ludgate Street glass factory. At the time of its original establishment around 1810, Jackson's business had been limited to the cutting and decorating of bought-in blank tableware, but the construction of a furnace and cone in 1836 gave Jackson the facility to blow his own glass. There were no skilled Blowers in the village at that time and the succeeding years saw an influx into Tutbury of qualified men from major glass centres around the country including Stourbridge in the Black Country, Warrington, Newcastle and Scotland.

Sivewright worked as an employee of the Jackson family until the early 1860's. He was also a lay Preacher, in whatever spare moments remained from his full-time job as a glassmaker combined with an almost equally full-time role as a local and national Trade Union organiser. This diversion of his energies may explain why, surprisingly, he does not appear to have reached the top shop-floor position of "Workman" within the classical four-man "Chair" into which glass-blowing teams were organised, but remained at the second-tier level of "Servitor".

He played a leading role in the early struggles to create a stable and effective trade union for Glass Blowers. The Flint Glass Makers' Friendly Society ("FGMFS") was established under Friendly Society legislation, and its ostensible purpose was to provide sickness, unemployment, death and eventually retirement benefits for members, in return for their modest fortnightly monetary contributions.

The Society also operated a system to match unemployed workers with vacancies in the industry elsewhere around the country. Beyond this, however, they increasingly operated as a trade union in the broader sense, defending their members' interests as they saw them, seeking to maintain a closed shop, and supporting workers during strikes and employer lock-outs.

The physical and intellectual energy required of a national organiser such as Sivewright in his position as Central Secretary ("CS") of the FGMFS was immense. Fuller details of his Trade Union career can be found in the sister volume to this publication, on the history of Tutbury Glassworks. His most lasting memorial is to be found in the pages of the Society's quarterly journal, The Flint Glass Makers' Magazine ("FGMM"), to which he was a significant founding contributor, later serving as Editor from 1860-63. The FGMM was the evidence on which the Socialist historians, Sidney and Beatrice Webb, ranked the Glass Blowers among the Victorian "Labour Aristocracy". William Alexander Sivewright helped set the educated tone of the magazine in its earliest days.

His sons William junior and John Hunter Sivewright had joined him in the Ludgate Street glass-blowing cone by 1851, aged twenty-one and thirteen respectively. By 1861 William junior was working as a Traveller for the Tutbury factory. John was also working as a salesman, but had changed industries to become a Brewer's Agent.

* * * * *

William Alexander Sivewright in Hatton - the Evidence

Only limited direct documentary proof has yet come to light to confirm Sivewright's occupation of the Scropton Lane site. But there is significant circumstantial and anecdotal support to place him as the first glass manufacturer in Hatton, blowing and cutting flint glass tableware from approximately 1863 to 1868 in what was first known as "the New Glassworks". Chronologically, what has been established with some certainty is as follows:

• Surviving local Trade Directories before the 1860's contain no references to any glass industry in Hatton.

• On the 1861 and earlier Censuses, there was only a small handful of glassworkers living in the parishes on the north side of the River Dove, drawn there, it seems, by domestic circumstances rather than the presence of any industry. For example, in 1861 Glass Blower John Chapman lived in Scropton village with his Scropton-born wife Hannah. And Blower Benjamin Poyner was living in Marston-on-Dove from 1851 to 1871 with his wife Matilda, born in nearby Hilton. In Hatton itself, back in 1851 we find only William Middleton, a 33-year-old Glass Cutter, and in 1841 four teenage Cutters and Apprentices. It is likely that all these were working at the Tutbury factory, and they should not be seen as evidence that glassmaking was taking place in Hatton at those times.

• In the summer of 1863 Sivewright wrote in the FGMM that he was obliged to resign from both his office as Central Secretary of the trade union and from active membership of the FGMFS itself: *"My present position of course precludes me from continuing to take any active part in the affairs of the society but if permitted to do so, I shall be glad to be identified with it as an Honorary Member."* In the context of the evidence that follows, it is clear that he was leaving the shopfloor and setting up in business himself.

• The early 1860's was a period of generally buoyant conditions in the glass trade, in retrospect one of its golden ages, and a promising environment for the establishment of new businesses in the industry.

Both William senior and junior had considerable exposure to the glass trade across the country, and the opportunity to try their own hand in business would have been tempting.

• Earlier in 1863 Eleanor Jackson had recruited the energetic JTH Richardson to manage the Ludgate Street factory. (Her husband Henry had died in 1849, leaving the business to Eleanor and her two spinster daughters Caroline and Mary Ann.) Whether the young Stourbridge "incomer" Richardson was initially well received on the shop-floor is not known. However, Sivewright's illustrious Union career must have given him considerable stature among his fellow workers, and confidence that a number of them would follow him if he decided to set up on his own.

• The New Scropton Lane area was undeveloped at the time, and was a "greenfield" site. The most contemporaneous map of the area (O.S.1st Edition 6" to One-mile, surveyed 1879-81) shows just the Glassworks and no other commercial buildings. Adjoining it is an orchard, and the rest is agricultural land. (See Chapter 3). It would have been an attractive location compared to Ludgate Street - open, level and next to the railway - and the only disadvantage may have been the potential risk of flooding from the nearby River Dove.

• In April 1864 the Tutbury Glass Works advertised in the Birmingham Gazette for twelve Flint Glass Cutters. This sizeable requirement is unlikely to reflect just internal expansion, and is more probably a reaction to the loss of skilled men to Sivewright's new venture. In December of that year, there was a further vacancy in Tutbury for a *"first-class wine chair"*, the advertisement quoting pay rates for Workman, Servitor and Footman. (Together with a boy "Taker-in", these three posts made up the traditional glass-blowing team or "Chair".) Then in March 1866, in the same newspaper, seven additional Cutters were sought for the Ludgate Street factory.

• In 1865 the Tutbury District membership of the FGMFS increased sharply to thirty-six from its historical level of around twenty-four, and then rose to over fifty in 1866/67. The FGMFS sought to operate a "closed shop" for Glass Blowers with a considerable degree of success (separate Unions existed for Glass Cutters), and so Union membership numbers are an excellent indicator of employment levels. This doubling of the local Blowing workforce in just three years is more easily explainable as the result of the establishment of a rival second business in Hatton than of organic growth in Ludgate Street.

• According to a report in the Derby Mercury in September 1866, Joseph Brown, a Glass Cutter of Hatton, was charged by PC Thorpe with being drunk and riotous in Hatton. This is the first known reference to a glassworker residing in Hatton in the 1860's.

• The 1868 Post Office Directory of Staffordshire listed in its Tutbury section *"Sivewright, William Alexander & Son, Flint glass manufacturers"*. Unfortunately, no address is given. But as indicated in the Introduction, Hatton was then included within the Tutbury postal district, and businesses located in Hatton figured in Staffordshire rather than Derbyshire commercial directories. There is no entry in the preceding 1863 edition. The "son" referred to was William Sivewright junior, as his younger brother John had emigrated in 1863.

• The first sign of difficulty for the business appears in the FGMM in Spring 1868 when the Central Committee reported: *"In April, we found it necessary to send a deputation to the Tutbury District, relative to men being discharged in what appeared an unsatisfactory manner, and after interviews with both the men and the employer, the notice of the men then under notice was withdrawn."* It is not clear which of the two Tutbury/Hatton establishments the proposed discharges related to, but subsequent events suggest that it was almost certainly the Scropton Lane factory.

- Shortly afterwards the London Gazette reported: *"William Alexander Sivewright and William Sivewright, of Tutbury, in the county of Stafford, Flint Glass Manufacturers and Copartners, having been adjudged bankrupts under a Petition, filed in Her Majesty's Court of Bankruptcy for the Birmingham District, on the 26th day of May, 1868, are hereby required to surrender themselves to Owen Davies Tudor, a Registrar of the said Court, at the first meeting of creditors to be held before the said Registrar, on the 12th day of June next, at twelve o'clock at noon precisely, at the said Court, at Birmingham."*

- In the week of 30th June 1868 seven Workmen joined the unemployed list of the FGMFS Tutbury District, followed a week later by another Workman plus nine Servitors and Footmakers. If this was the entirety of the workforce of the Hatton Blowing Shop, it would imply eight "chairs" working perhaps an eight-pot furnace on a double shift basis, with the support of boys and apprentices (who were not eligible for Union membership). Whilst some of the redundant Workmen were relative newcomers to the locality, several others (Philip McGuiness, Benjamin Bell, Benjamin Smart and George Cooke) were long-standing Tutbury stalwarts, evidence that Sivewright had been able to take some of the Jacksons' best craftsmen with him from Ludgate Street after 1863.

- The bankruptcy was finalised quickly. The Birmingham Journal reported that on 17th July 1868 a final hearing was held and the Sivewrights were discharged.

- Harrod & Co's 1870 Commercial Directory listed "William Livewright" [sic] residing in High Street, Tutbury, operating a Wholesale Glass Warehouse, and his son, also William "Livewright" of Burton Road, working as a Commercial Traveller.

- On the April 1871 Census William senior was living in High Street,

Tutbury, his occupation Glass Merchant - probably just trying to scrape a living as a dealer from the remnants of his business. His son had left the area and by 1881 was working as a Glass Agent in London. He later followed his brother John and emigrated with his family to Australia in 1885.

• Also on the 1871 Census, the residence of Clara and Thomas Wardle, a railway porter, was given as "Glass Works", Old Scropton Lane. The Wardles may have been acting as caretakers of the then disused factory, living in what appears to have been a small dwelling house in the south-west corner of the site, shown in this wintry scene of dereliction after Trent Valley's final closure in the 1980's.

Figure 3 - The Wardle's Cottage?

• On 2nd July 1872 William Alexander Sivewright was buried at St Mary's, Tutbury aged 61. He does not appear to have left a will or a surviving gravestone. No death notice or obituary has been found in local newspapers or in the FGMM.

- In 1955 former RCGW employee Mr Frank Pegg, then in his early seventies, passed on his knowledge of the origins of the Hatton factory to Mr WH Bennett, the managing director of Trent Valley Glassworks. Mr Pegg stated that *"The Hatton Works were built for a Mr Sivewright and used by him for the manufacture of tableware. Later the works were acquired by Thomas Haden Richardson..."* How reliable is Mr Pegg's information? Born in 1883, he followed his father George's trade as an Engineering Fitter. In 1910 he was employed in this role at the Hatton Glassworks, recently re-opened by George Harry Corbett. Back in April 1901 both he and his father were living in Hatton and working as Fitters, though it is not clear if this was at the Glassworks which was closed around that time. In 1891 his father had been living in Burton Street, Tutbury, working as a Blacksmith - quite possibly at the Tutbury Glassworks which frequently employed its own Smith.

From this it is clear that Frank Pegg would have overlapped in the local industry with men who had been involved in the earliest days of the Hatton Works. An example is Benjamin Bell, one of the men who lost their job at the time of Sivewright's bankruptcy in 1868, and who in 1901 was still working at the Tutbury Glassworks. And, of course, JTH Richardson himself was prominent in the local industry from the early 1860's to the first years of the twentieth century and would have been well aware of the origins of the Scropton Lane operation that he took on in 1871. There is therefore no reason to doubt that Mr Pegg's information, though second hand, would have come from knowledgeable sources.

* * * * *

Sivewright in Hatton - What Remains to be Discovered?

Large gaps in the picture of this first phase of Hatton glassmaking remain:

• The extent of the physical set-up of Sivewright's Works is not yet certain. At first sight, it would be rather surprising if Sivewright could have financed something quite as substantial as the Royal Castle Glass Works complex shown on this book's front cover and that first appeared as an engraving in an advertisement by JTH Richardson in the Pottery Gazette and Glass Trade Review of October 1879 (see Chapter 3). A more likely assumption would be that Sivewright operated from something more modest in the 1860's and that Richardson expanded the factory substantially in the following decade, perhaps using access to family or industry funds in Stourbridge.

However, this photograph of Hatton Glassworks has recently come to light in the files of the National Archives at Kew. It is by some decades the earliest known real-life image of the factory.

Figure 4 - "The New Glassworks"

18

The photograph was the subject of a Memorandum for Registration of Copyright under the Copyright (Works of Art) Act by a Joseph Roberts of nearby Sudbury, Derbyshire, made in October 1880. (Joseph Roberts is listed in Harrod's 1870 Directory as a Beer Retailer and Photographer in Draycott-in-the Clay, near Sudbury, though 1871 and later Censuses describe him solely as a publican.)

The view is taken from ground level and slightly to the right of that adopted in the engraving, but the majority of the building elements in the two documents can be closely matched. However, playing "spot the difference", a number of things do emerge:

- The photograph shows two furnace chimneys, the engraving has three in one version and four in another.
- In the engraving, the central two storey building, probably a Cutting Shop, has roof lights, the photograph has none.
- In the engraving, there are three storeys of windows to the apex-fronted middle block, whilst the photograph has only ground floor windows at that point; there is also a difference in roofline.
- The copyright application refers to the property as the "New Glassworks, Hatton", whereas Richardson referred to his factory as the Castle Glassworks from the moment he took over in 1871.

These differences all suggest that, despite the copyright registration not being made until 1880, the photograph could pre-date the 1879 engraving by some years. But how many years? Earlier in the 1870's or right back to Sivewright's time?

Another feature of the photograph stands out - where is everybody? The engraving conveys the bustle of industrial life, smoking chimneys, laden carts, employees hither and thither. The photograph is devoid of activity, almost sterile, not a person or beast in sight, no "stuff" lying around, no sign of the furnaces being alight – and no glassmaker ever let his furnace go out if it could be avoided. This suggests a third possibility – that the Glassworks was shut down and this photograph was in fact taken in the period between the Sivewrights' bankruptcy in 1868 and Richardson's re-opening in 1871. The line of reasoning is tempting, but it leads one to the currently unanswered question of where on earth did the Sivewrights find the money to build this?

With the possible exception of the change in colour of the roof-tiling on the left-hand building, the brickwork and building style appear "all of a piece", implying that the Works were not built in stages.

However, neither the photo nor the engraving really show the rear of the premises which is where, if Sivewright's Glassworks had only been a part of the later whole, one would expect it to have been situated.

The two furnace structures pictured here (before and after their demolition in September 1949) are at the rear of the site, by the railway line, looking to the west. One can say with more certainty perhaps that these at least do indeed date from Sivewright's time in the 1860's.

Figure 5 - Built in 1863?

The second photo from the 1949 demolition is a closer shot, from the same direction, as confirmed by the railway signal (which is faintly visible on the original of the first photo) and the elevated structure in the left centre of the picture (which is partially obscured by the chimney in the first photo). The partly demolished buildings seen in this second photo, which were previously obscured, are also likely to have been original.

Figure 6 – Demolished in 1949

Irrespective of the exact dating, there are other points of interest in the National Archive photograph:

- The suggested cottage of Mr and Mrs Wardle certainly has the appearance of a dwelling house.
- The "greenfield" nature of the site is very evident.

- The six-sided conical roof structure appears to be a shelter for straw; its sides are not present in the engraving.

• However large or small it may have been, it is not known if Sivewright owned or leased his premises. If Mr Pegg's words are taken literally, the Works "were built for Mr Sivewright", i.e., he did not take on an existing industrial building. The "New" in "New Glassworks" should probably be interpreted as relative to the existing Ludgate Street factory, rather than to an unknown earlier glassworks in Hatton.

• Little is known about the products, markets or customers, beyond that the business was making glass tableware. It is unlikely that Sivewright would have attempted anything greatly different to what he and his fellow Tutbury Blowers had been producing all their lives: wine and spirit glasses, fruit, sugar and salt bowls, decanters, flower vases, etc. – in blown lead crystal, decorated by cutting, etching and engraving. One beautiful and credibly authenticated example of their craft is now known, as will be seen at the end of this chapter.

• Whilst seventeen men from the Blowing Shop can be identified from FGMFS records, the size of the Cutting Shop is not known. Generally, in the local glass industry over the years, the sizes of the two workforces were similar. If so, together with ancillary workers, Sivewright was probably employing over forty people in total at the time of the factory's closure.

• The respective roles of Sivewright and his son are not known. From his previous and subsequent sales career, it is likely that William junior took the lead on the commercial side, and it would be logical for William senior to have run the factory. We do not know who was the real driving force behind the venture - in 1863 the father was aged fifty-two, the son thirty-three.

• Nothing is known of the financial set-up of the partnership. There is no indication that the Sivewrights were of other than relatively modest means. Before 1863, besides the two wages from Jackson's factory, the family had a grocery shop and at one time ran the local Post Office. William's stipend as FGMFS Secretary was no more than a token £30 a year. Did the partnership have financing from outside sources, both for the establishment of the factory in Scropton Lane and to provide an income to the partners in the development period till it was up and running?

Some financial information can be gleaned from the bankruptcy report. An initial deficiency of £3,089 had been recorded, with liabilities of £3,887 and assets of £798 (comprising trade debtors of £248 and "property given up" of £550). The liabilities included £1,333 of discounted bills of exchange, which had subsequently been paid. Trade creditor debts of £1,050 were also "withdraw[n] so far as the deficiency". The final deficiency was reduced to £798 and there were no objectors to the discharge. It seems that the partners did their best to resolve the losses, and did not cut and run.

For present-day equivalent values, one needs to apply a multiplier of about 50, which would give creditor and debtor figures within a range expected for a small/medium sized factory. There are no clues as to the factory building's ownership, neither the existence of a freehold asset nor liabilities under a mortgage or lease.

• The causes of the bankruptcy are unknown. Certainly, in Victorian times, glassmaking ventures came and went with bewildering rapidity. But there is no indication that 1867/8 was a period of any great depression in the trade. Perhaps the Sivewright partnership was under-capitalised from the start. And there are indications in the FGMM that careful bookkeeping had not been a forte of Sivewright's tenure as FGMFS Secretary.

Known for his diplomatic skills in the relatively structured environment of the trade union, maybe he lacked the ruthlessness to survive in the cut-throat world of an employer. And perhaps the Tutbury Glassworks, historically very price competitive, reacted ruthlessly itself to their new local rival.

* * * * *

William Alexander Sivewright - a Happier Ending?

Thus ended, in a short-lived four or five years, the first attempt at creating a glass-making industry in Hatton – indeed the first known sizeable industrial venture of any kind in the village.

Hopefully William Alexander Sivewright did not die a completely broken man. In the hectic later years of his life, he had helped end the most damaging national trade dispute in the glass industry's history, served a second three-year term at the head of his Union, and launched his own venture which he no doubt intended to run on the basis of enlightened relations with his workforce.

But simultaneously, he had seen his daughters, Ann and Martha, and daughter-in-law Mary buried at a young age in Tutbury, and bidden farewell to his younger son John who left these shores permanently for Australia with his family. Then, together with his elder son, he faced the ultimate Victorian disaster of bankruptcy.

However, though all but forgotten in Hatton and Tutbury until now, the legacy of William Alexander Sivewright, glassmaker, does happily survive in very concrete form on the opposite side of the world.

In 2014 this fine decanter was to be found in the unexpected setting of New Zealand's beautiful Coromandel Peninsula, home to descendants of his family. If family lore is correct, the piece comes from great-great grandfather Sivewright's glass factory. William's younger son, John H. Sivewright, emigrated to Australia in spring 1863, just before the factory opened, followed in 1885 by William Alexander's other surviving children,

Figure 7 - A well-travelled decanter

William jnr. and daughter Mary. It seems most likely that the decanter was among the possessions they took with them in 1885. John had five surviving daughters, all of whom later moved on to New Zealand, and the piece passed down through the family to the present generation.

The decoration in the panel is of a grape vine. The vertical stalk seems to be engraved, as are the leaf veins and grape stalks. The grapes and the leaves appear to be etched. On the basis of the provenance described above, the decanter is the only known work from the first period of the Hatton Glassworks.

* * * * *

3. 1871-1900 John Thomas Haden Richardson & Sons

Harrod & Co's 1870 Commercial Directory lists John T H Richardson as Manager of the Tutbury Flint Glass Company of High Street [sic], Tutbury, and on the April 1871 Census John Thos Richardson of Burton Street described himself as a Flint Glass Manufacturer employing 97 workers. No other Glassworks managers were living in the village, and from the size of the workforce it is clear that at the time of the Census he was still running the Ludgate Street factory for the Jackson family. Quite probably he was living in the Manager's house, Southernhey, situated just above the works on the west side of Burton Street.

But within the next two months Richardson left the Tutbury Glassworks and set up on his own account on the Scropton Lane site which had been out of production since the Sivewright bankruptcy in 1868.

John Thomas Haden Richardson was from a very different background to William Alexander Sivewright. Born in the Black Country in Wordsley, Staffordshire on 14th January 1835, he came from one of the most famous dynasties of Stourbridge glassmakers. His father Jonathon Richardson, together with the latter's elder brothers Benjamin and William, were at the forefront of the Stourbridge industry's spectacular advances in the early Victorian era. They were in turn the sons of Joseph Richardson, who had been the leading furnace cone builder in the area, and his wife Martha nee Haden. In partnership from 1842 as "W.H., B. and J. Richardson, Glassmakers", the brothers capitalised on the development opportunities provided by the 1845 repeal of the unpopular Glass Excise Tax, which had previously stifled innovation and enterprise in the English glass manufacturing trade.

Benjamin Richardson was the real driving force, initiating successful experiments in coloured glass, pressed glass, cased glass, vitrified enamel glass, acid etching and much more. The partnership was awarded the Royal Society of Arts' Gold Medal in 1847, and exhibited prominently at the Crystal Palace Great Exhibition of 1851, the trade's finest showcase. There were financial difficulties along the way, but Benjamin's technical endeavours continued to flourish into the 1860's. Several of the most renowned Stourbridge craftsmen of the following generation learnt their trade with the Richardsons, including William Muckley, Philip Pargeter and John Northwood.

It must have been something of a coup for Eleanor Jackson to secure the services of John Thomas Haden Richardson for her Tutbury factory, to succeed a series of what had probably been less than satisfactory managers following the death of her husband Henry Jackson in 1849. Richardson had taken up a position in Tutbury by 1863 when the Post Office Directory of Staffordshire listed *"Tutbury Glass Company, flint glass manufacturers of every description (J T H Richardson, Manager)."* The business at the time of his arrival appears to have been a partnership between Eleanor and her daughters. By the time of the next edition of the Directory in 1868 Richardson was (or was describing himself as) "Managing Partner". His precise financial arrangements with the Jackson family across the period are not known.

What were Richardson's motives for coming to Tutbury? He had been brought up in comfortable family surroundings, and schooled until at least the age of sixteen. His father had died in 1857, and by the 1861 Census John was a Commercial Traveller in Glass, aged 26, lodging close to a glassworks in Gateshead on Tyneside, probably travelling on behalf of the family firm back in Stourbridge, where no doubt his Uncle Benjamin still ruled the roost. He was married two years later in Wordsley to Sarah Richards, some eight years older than him, daughter of a local Saddler. One can only surmise that he thought the Tutbury business offered more responsibility and opportunity than his own family's firm. But there must have been other alternative career paths available for a young man so well-connected in the extensive West Midlands glass trade, rather than a move to the isolated backwater of Tutbury. Indeed, Tutbury's connections with Stourbridge at the time appear to have been closer at the Union level than between employers. Was John deliberately thumbing his nose at his uncle by joining the factory of Henry Jackson whom Benjamin had raged against twenty years earlier as "the curse of the trade" because of his price-cutting tactics? Or was it all a cunning Stourbridge plan to bring the troublesome Tutbury business under their control?

Whatever his motivation, Richardson's nine-year tenure in charge of the Tutbury Glassworks was relatively successful. The departure to Hatton of Sivewright, followed by many of his best craftsmen, was a baptism of fire. But employment levels at Tutbury increased over the period, labour relations were generally quiet, there were innovations in the product range and production processes, and he eventually saw off the competition of Sivewright's venture.

We do not know how mutually satisfactory the relations were between him and the Jackson ladies. But, approaching early middle age in 1871, he clearly decided that he could do better for himself by setting up on his own account, and left to resurrect the Scropton Lane works. It was the start of an operation that ran for almost thirty years.

The picture of Richardson's operation that has survived is less fragmentary than that of Sivewright's. It is can be usefully characterised by taking the ten-yearly national Censuses as boundary markers for three decades of contrasting fortunes for the business.

* * * * *

The Royal Castle Glass Works 1871-81: Resurrection and Growth

• In the Birmingham Daily Post of 27th June 1871, the earliest known reference to the Castle Glassworks appeared in this advertisement: *"Flint Glass Trade. Packer wanted. One accustomed to take off Goods in Lear preferred. Apply, stating age, wages, and where last employed, to Mr J T H Richardson, Castle Flint Glass Works, Tutbury, Staffordshire."* No other Castle Glassworks recruitment adverts from this initial period have yet come to light, which suggests that Richardson either enticed a very substantial number of men away from the Tutbury Glassworks, or was able to recruit through word of mouth via his trade contacts in Stourbridge and elsewhere, or utilized the unemployed register of the FGMFS.

• By August 1871 membership of the FGMFS Tutbury District had increased to forty-three, and then in the following quarters to around fifty, at which level it stabilized for several years. This was from a low point of thirty in 1869 after Sivewright's closure. (Hatton never became a District of the Union in its own right, and the Blowers working there were included in the Tutbury District numbers).

• The 1872 Post Office Directory of Staffordshire lists in its Tutbury section *"John Thomas Haden Richardson, Flint Glass Manufacturer, Castle Glassworks."* (Jabez Elton had taken over as manager of the Tutbury Glass Company by then). There are similar subsequent entries in the Directories of 1876, 1880, 1884, 1888, 1892 and 1896. C N Wright's 1874 Directory of South Derbyshire also includes it, more helpfully, in its Hatton section.

• The 1972 Centenary History of Tutbury Cricket Club records a match in 1874 between Mr Richardson's "Tutbury Glass Coy" and "The Minnows", "on a ground at the corner of Scropton Lane and Station Road, Hatton", the Minnows making 44 runs and the

29

Glassworkers 41. In July 1877 a further match took place on "Mr Mason's field" between Tutbury Mill's second eleven and the Castle Glassworks. Conditions on Mr Mason's field no doubt continued to be a little rough and favoured the bowlers, as over two innings the Mill amassed just 103 runs, whilst the Glassworks managed a paltry 15 in their first innings, though a more respectable 73 in the second. The Glassworks players were G Woolley, J Bell, T Champion, W Kenyon, A Smith, J Freeman, E Bennett, J Oakton, J Woolley, G Worrall and A Moorcroft, mostly lads in their teens, with some well-known Tutbury glassmaking names amongst them.

• On 5th May 1878 the Derby Mercury advertised: "*Flint Glass Cutters. Wanted, Youths who have served part of their time and left their employers through depression of trade. Apply to Mr Richardson, Castle Glassworks, Tutbury, near Burton-on-Trent.*"

• By 1878 amazing things were happening in Hatton. The Editor of The Pottery and Glass Trades Journal noted in its December edition:

"I have... seen two magnificent trumpet vases, which were manufactured ... by Mr J T H Richardson of Hatton. I remember a vase of the kind some ten feet in height, which was exhibited by Messrs. Hodgetts, Richardson and Co. at the late Exhibition at Paris, and which attracted much attention there as being a marvellous specimen of glass-blowing.

One of the vases which Mr Richardson has succeeded in turning out is fourteen feet in height without the foot, thirty inches in diameter at the top, and one and a half inches in diameter at the socket. It is without exception the largest and finest article of the kind ever blown. The stem is perfectly straight and the metal free from the many imperfections to which such a large piece of blown glass is liable."

- Richardson was advertising regularly in the Journal by then and from October 1879 onwards his adverts included an engraving of the Works, on behalf of *"J.T.H. Richardson. By Royal Letters Patent. Royal Castle Flint Glass Works, Hatton near Burton-on-Trent, Staffordshire, Manufacturers of all kinds of Flint, Emerald & Ruby Glass, Cut & Engraved, for Home and Export Trade. London Show Room: Ely House, Charterhouse St, Holborn Circus."* It is probably the single most informative document about the 19th century Hatton Glassworks.

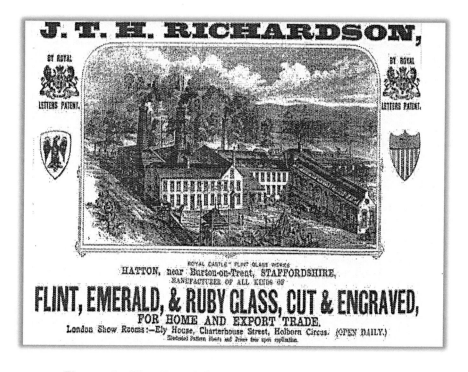

Figure 8 - The Royal Castle Flint Glass Works 1879

The engraving was still being used, with minor modifications, on RCGW letterhead in 1911. The image definition in that version is much sharper and is also reproduced below.

31

Figure 9 – Unchanged, 30 Years on

From the advertisement and illustration, one can deduce the following:

- The view is from an imagined elevated position on New Scropton Lane, looking south, with Tutbury Castle and the Needwood Forest escarpment in the distance. The Works are quite substantial, even allowing for the Victorian engraver's habitual skill in portraying the humblest factory as a grandiose industrial complex.

- There are several sections to the Works. To the left rear lies the Blowing House, with two circular furnace chimneys rising from the roof spaces, plus a third whose base is unseen. There are no broad cones in the style of that built at Jackson's Tutbury factory in 1836. A smaller square chimney stands to the rear. To the front of the Blowing House is a two storied, twelve-bay building, with an eight-bay building of identical style set back from it - they both have a large number of windows, plus roof lights in the second one, and no doubt included the Cutting Shops. A small single storey building sits in the angle

32

formed by them - possibly a reception and counting house. A long single-storey structure runs at right angles to the main buildings - a horse and cart are lined up at its entrance and it was probably in use as a store for raw materials, pots or finished goods.

- The North Staffordshire Railway line runs alongside the rear of the factory. The layout of the buildings closely matches that shown on the most contemporaneous local map:

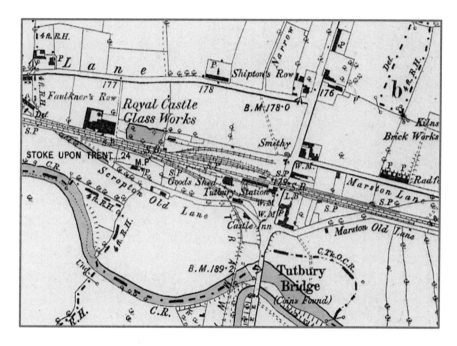

Figure 10 - Royal Castle Glass Works site c.1880
*Ordnance Survey 1st Edition six-inch map Sheet L111 SE extract
(surveyed 1879-81, published 1883).*

- Richardson's product range is set out in the advertisement: cut and engraved flint, emerald and ruby glass. He has a London showroom in Holborn, the centre of the capital's wholesale and retail glass trade, and also some export business.

33

- Finally, and unexpectedly, Richardson has already adopted the name of "Royal Castle Flint Glass Works" by 1879. This decisively contradicts the frequently repeated assertion that the "Royal" designation arose after a visit to the factory in 1899 (1897 in some sources) by the Duke and Duchess of York, (later King George V and Queen Mary). An 1899 visit by the Duchess did indeed take place, a successful and well-remembered one, but it is clear that Richardson's adoption of the adjective came at a much earlier date. The phrase "By Royal Letters Patent" would be a reference to inventions or production processes that Richardson had patented, and should not be confused with the modern Royal Warrant, whereby goods are supplied to the Royal Family. The use of the term "Royal" for business purposes is tightly constrained today under the Trade Marks Act 1994. To what extent Richardson had permission for the name or was just indulging in a cheeky bit of marketing, one can only speculate. The Castle certainly had royal connections, but the Works…? Nevertheless, consent or no consent, that did not diminish the commercial impact and cachet which endured for many years.

• On the 1881 Census 118 inhabitants can be identified as employed in the glass industry in the Tutbury area. These include twelve living in Hatton and one in Marston-on-Dove, with the rest in Tutbury itself. John T H Richardson was now living in Scropton Road. The next entries to his house in the Census are for properties in Old Scropton Lane, where the Glassworks had been recorded in 1871, so it is probable that his house was either on or adjoining the factory site (as was the case with the Tutbury manager's house). He gave his occupation as Flint Glass Manufacturer, employing a total of 60 people - 30 men, 27 boys and 3 women. (By implication, the Ludgate Street factory, recently re-opened after a brief closure in 1880, had a similar size of workforce). Aged 46, he must have been in the prime of his life. His three children, Frederick aged 17, Thomas aged 15 and Katie aged 12, all born in Tutbury shortly after his arrival from

Stourbridge, were at home along with their mother and one domestic servant - a relatively modest household. The children had no occupation listed, and the boys may still have been in education.

It is a little surprising that Frederick and Thomas, though only thirteen and eleven at the time, did not appear along with their father's young employees in the cricket matches referred to earlier, as Thomas in particular was to become an accomplished cricketer. Tom Coxon, historian of the local cricket club, recalled: *"In 1877 Tom Richardson made his first appearance for Tutbury and played until the 1920s. I remember him making 54 not out against Denstone College in 1922. He also played for Staffordshire and Derbyshire."* A right-handed batsman, he made his initial first-class appearance in 1888, playing in an England XI against a team of touring Australians. A local cricketing poet penned the following words about the two brothers in 1891:

"Of Fred and Tom, the brothers tall,
Who come from Hatton town:
This ditty of the bat and ball
Their merits full shall own.

Tom very seldom joins his team,
He wanders far and wide;
He goes, 'tis said, along the stream,
Where 'lunch' the swells provide.

But still he always turns up trumps,
He's strong on every point;
He bowls and bats, he fields and stumps,
He hits and fears them not.

In County play he's made his mark,
And's often picked to play;
And once, against the Australians,
His prowess made display.

Fred shines the best in field, at point,
His batting is not strong;
But frequently his stand has stopped
The Club from going wrong.

He's always ready, too, to give
A helping hand with ground;
His strength with scythe is, as I live,
A cure for thistles, sound.

He helps to put the chains up firm,
When others say 'Good-night!'
And with the Secretary trim
Packs all away quite right."

Frederick was clearly in his younger brother's shadow on the cricket field. We do not know if this was the case in other aspects of their relationship.

• Returning to the 1881 Census, three doors away from the Richardsons lived Frederick August Bohm aged 32, a Glass Engraver and Etcher, born in Bohemia, together with his Wordsley-born wife. Glass engraving was a Bohemian speciality. Bohm was one of a number of highly skilled engravers from that region who had found their way in the 1860's to the Stourbridge area. Richardson recruited Bohm initially for the Tutbury factory, from where the young man followed him to Hatton. Bohm was probably used to train local men in the art of engraving, though Richardson advertised for an additional Engraver in the Birmingham Post in April 1874. By the time of the 1891 Census Bohm and his family were living modestly in Blackpool Street in Burton-on-Trent. His occupation was still Glass Engraver, but it is not clear if he remained working for the Hatton or Tutbury factories or was by then self-employed. A fine example of his work is shown in Chapter 5.

• Whilst the twelve glassworkers living in Hatton in 1881 are likely to have been amongst those employed at the Hatton factory, it is not possible from the Census alone to identify which of the Tutbury residents make up the rest of the Hatton workforce. However, as has been stated, it seems very probable that Richardson would have taken a number of the best men from the Tutbury Glassworks with him when he set up in 1871. And as regards the Blowers amongst them, later Union reports allow the RCGW workers to be identified, as will be seen below.

* * * * *

Figure 11 – FGMFS Membership Certificate

• Later in 1881 an episode occurred that portrays Richardson in a very different light from the reasonable and complaisant employer that received an FGMFS delegation to Tutbury Glassworks in 1869 to negotiate the operation of a new wine glass shearing machine of his design. It seems that the custom in the trade was that if poor glass was blown, the blowers didn't get paid for it, but that it was then to be broken up for cullet. By 1881 Richardson was not only being very picky about what he classified as bad glass, but instead of breaking it all up he was taking much of it into store and selling it as seconds, without paying the blowers anything. The men reported this to the Union, who considered it an important test-case about the importance of "custom" in the trade. With Union approval, the Hatton men set about breaking a token amount of the glass in protest. Richardson called in the local Bobby and tried to get the men imprisoned for criminal damage.

The case was heard before the Magistrates in Sudbury. There is a very readable FGMM report by the Union Central Secretary, Tom Barnes, on the outcome of the hearing. Part of the report is shown in Appendix A, as an excellent example of the impressive language and sentiments characteristic of the FGMM. Barnes, together with the Union's advocate, made his way by rail from Birmingham New Street to Burton Station and then on by road to Sudbury - via the bar of the Castle Inn where he found the men in good spirits. It appears that the Magistrates joined in the opprobrium that was being heaped on Richardson by the Union. It was a happy group that returned to Tutbury later that day, as the Burton Chronicle reported:

"TUTBURY. The usual quiet and calm monotony of our village was enlivened on the afternoon of Monday 31st inst., by the sounds of shouting and cheering, gun-firing, etc, the perpetrators thereof being a party of glassblowers returning from Sudbury, and the raison d'etre being a victory over their masters."

Although the blowers aren't named in the FGMM report, it seems likely that the lead in this affair would have been taken by Edward Bentley, the Tutbury District Secretary and Treasurer, and Benjamin Bell, the District President and most senior Blower at the RCGW at the time. Barnes and the men congratulated themselves on not subsequently taking *"advantage of their Employer as he had taken advantage of them"*, and acting magnanimously in victory. But did the episode sour relations in the years to come? In attempting to understand Richardson's unacceptable behaviour, the most obvious factor is that the buoyant trading times of 1869 were changing radically by 1881, with a severe and prolonged trade depression that had provoked the closure of the Jacksons' Tutbury Glassworks a year before. Richardson, like the rest of the industry, was just trying to survive.

• An answer to the question of future relations soon came at the end of 1882. The FGMM reported turbulent times at Richardson's Works. The factory closed down in October, because of a reported shortage of work. Within a few weeks Richardson re-opened on a limited basis, using "black" labour and different operating practices. The Tutbury FGMFS District was in uproar, partly against Richardson but more vehemently (as was invariably the case) against two of their colleagues, S. Husselbee and J. Woolley, who had "gone black".

The District's Report to the FGMM is signed by probably all the members of the District. Taken together with the Unemployment Reports of the FGMFS, which show a sharp increase in men out of work in the District from the week of 7th October 1882, it is possible to identify and split the local blowing workforce between those working in Ludgate Street and those in Scropton Lane. The thirteen men left out of work by the RCGW closure were Workmen B. Bell, J. Griffin, W. Downey, W. Kay and J. Woolley; Servitors S. Husselbee, W. Woolley, W. Sturgess, A. Donkin and J. Freeman; Footmakers J.

Griffin, G. Woolley and C. Pincher. With Takers-in, they would have formed four Chairs.

• The FGMM tracked the progress of the confrontation. In January 1883: *"We have to report that Mr Richardson of Tutbury has started a small furnace, and if all be true we hear is going to work as an iron glass-blower, and so revolutionise the Trade. Two of his old men have gone in "Black" and are working against all instructions of the Officers and District.* Three months later, in April 1883: *" Mr Richardson of Tutbury, we are sorry to say, is doing all in his power to fill his place with black sheep, to enable him to carry on, but from what we hear he will soon get tired of them, as we know the quality of the men he has got, and also the principles under which they are working."* Clearly Richardson was in difficulties, trying to find some way to cut his operating costs. But it is hard not to conclude that he was also looking to take some revenge on the Union for his humiliation before the Sudbury magistrates a year earlier.

There followed something of a stand-off. The District reported the following quarter that they had stopped the unemployment pay of *"J Freeman, gone in black"* The Union Secretary Barnes and one of the Central Committee members came to Tutbury, to persuade other men against similar action. The local unemployed men remained unemployed for many months, eventually at the reduced weekly unemployment pay of 2/-, until they drifted off to work elsewhere - most of the senior men went under the Union's redirection of labour scheme, to Birmingham, Stourbridge, Manchester and London.

(It is noticeable how frequently Secretary Barnes, and his other West Midlands-based predecessors, found reason to make a visit to out-of-the-way Tutbury on Union affairs. A day out to our rural idyll away from the Black Country grime, expenses and wages paid, clearly had its attractions.)

The FGMFS committee were further incensed when blacklegs Husselbee and Woolley started an action through Stone and Mole, Derby Solicitors, against the Society for the return of their lifelong contributions of £79 and £58 respectively. The Society vigorously rejected this novel, potentially floodgate-opening claim, both in principle and on the basis that Husselbee had received at least £66 back in benefits over the period of his membership. Nothing further was ever heard, though the Society did cover itself against similar future problems by quickly amending its Rule Book to specifically exclude such claims. The following year Husselbee, *"a man who has done more than any man in the last five years to try and corrupt and ruin the trade"*, turned up as a strike-breaker in a long-running dispute at Stones in Birmingham and, notwithstanding, put in an application to rejoin the FGMFS, to which the Society gave short shrift.

• At the beginning of 1884, the Union Central Committee continued to aim their sarcasm at Richardson: *"We have yet to learn of the threat of a Tutbury manufacturer that he was going to revolutionize the whole trade and place the Society in a heap of ruins. This, most certainly, has not yet taken place, nor, we are bound to say, from what we can see, is there any immediate likelihood."* Despite these fighting words, the Union's Tutbury District was now in a sad way. By May 1884 it had just fourteen employed, contributing members (all working at the Tutbury Glass Company), plus six retired members in receipt of a Union pension, and four men in receipt of unemployment pay. The District was in a permanent financial deficit at these levels, with the cost of the pension and unemployment payments outweighing the contributions made each quarter, such that the District had to be regularly supported from central funds.

• Fortunately, for both sides, peace did eventually break out. In January 1886 the Union's Central Committee was able to say: "*One of the good things we have to report is that we have arranged with Mr*

Richardson of Tutbury, to supply him with hands, and we are told by the Secretary that he is preparing for this change. After a long struggle we have become once more friends, and the Members of the District have vindicated their rights. We would add that the District Secretary deserves well of his District and the Trade for the assistance rendered to the Executive in this matter. We trust that a more united and better feeling will now prevail, and that Mr Richardson's Factory will be a good place of work once more."

The measured and non-triumphalist tone suggests that compromises were made on both sides, in the context of a continuing severe depression both in the glass industry and in world trade generally. Evidence of the settlement can be seen in the District's Quarterly Return. Ten new members joined the District roll on December 17th 1885: John Woolley (aged 37), John Homer (40), Edward Sage (40), Herbert Mear (40), Ben Ryder (37), Richard Cooksey (27), George Woolley (24), James Woolley (21) and John Pye (23). The District membership surged back up to thirty-five, and the local Union finances came back close to equilibrium. It seems that the forgiveness even extended to John Woolley, almost certainly the previously vilified blackleg "J. Woolley". This is our third acquaintance with his younger brother, the photographically ubiquitous George Woolley, who later unwittingly makes a vital contribution to the interpretation of the succeeding twenty-five years history through his fondness for appearing on camera.

The repercussions within the village of a prolonged dispute such as happened at the RCGW from 1882 to 1885 can easily be imagined. Men had to leave their homes and families, and travel to often distant parts of the country to find work within the trade. Whilst a temporary job in Birmingham or Stourbridge was close enough to have allowed occasional weekend contact with their families, work in Manchester, London or Scotland could bring with it separation on a very different scale. But it may be wrong to condemn the blacklegs outright - the short-term cushion of unemployment pay from the FGMFS was barely enough to keep a man's family from destitution, and the sacrifices asked of them in the struggle to maintain their Union's restrictive working practices and pay structures were something that not all had the single-mindedness to sustain. To carry on working in face of the hostility of their peers required a form of courage as well.

- Below is an 1884 Apprentice Indenture:

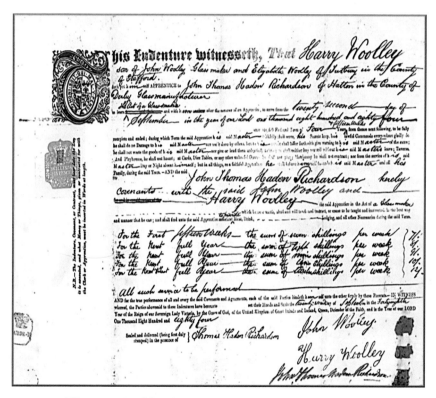

Figure 12 - Signing one's teenage years away

The Indenture is between Harry Woolley, son of John Woolley, himself a Glassmaker of Tutbury, and John Thomas Haden

Richardson of Hatton, Glass Manufacturer, *"to learn the Art of a Glassmaker".*

The apprenticeship was for four years and fifteen weeks at a weekly wage of seven shillings rising by annual increments to twelve shillings. The Indenture was witnessed by Richardson's son Thomas. It has the strict constraints on the apprentice's personal behaviour which were typical of the time: *"Taverns and Playhouses he shall not haunt; at Cards, Dice Tables, or any other unlawful Games he shall not play; Matrimony he shall not contract; nor from the services of his said Master Day or Night absent himself."* Absence from work on the part of an apprentice could be punished quite disproportionately - Thomas Woolley, a Tutbury Glass Company Apprentice in 1873 was given a month in prison for just that. Harry was sixteen at this time. He served his time and the indenture was endorsed *"Well and faithfully served"* in January 1889, signed by JTH Richardson.

The Indenture was entered into in the last days of the long RCGW dispute. Despite the large number of Woolleys in the local industry, there is little doubt that Harry's father, John, was the "black sheep" J Woolley. John Woolley lived to the age of 83 and, if his 1933 Burton Chronicle obituary is to be believed, came to be regarded as one of the grand old men of the village, whose residents learned of his passing *"with deep regret..., a delightful companion to the last, being full of the joy and vim of life, and he possessed in marked degree a kind heart and humorous disposition."* Clearly, earlier differences were forgotten by most as the years passed. Amongst his many interests and talents, he had been a keen sportsman in his younger days, a well-known runner and a sparring partner to Bob Brettell, a renowned Tutbury boxer - perhaps a clean pair of heels and a sharp pair of fists had been useful attributes in distant times when his popularity in the village had been less in evidence.

44

- In May 1887 Richardson tried his luck again with the legal system, when the Chancery Division of the High Court heard the case of Richardson v Castry and Gee. The Stourbridge, Brierley Hill and County Express reported: *"The action was brought by Mr Richardson, a glass manufacturer residing at Hatton in Derbyshire, and he sought to restrain the defendants, who are also glass manufacturers carrying on business at Amblecote, from infringing the plaintiff's patent apparatus for the improved manufacture of wine glass "feet", known as mull wines. The invention in question, it appeared, was an arrangement of boards, with a handle, a spring and loop, which enabled the glassblower to mould the feet of wine glasses without the assistance of a boy, as had been done heretofore; and it was also claimed for the patent that the wine-glass feet were made with greater rapidity, with greater finish, and were lighter, therefore consuming less metal in their manufacture."*

Richardson had taken out his patent in April 1876, but claimed that the infringement only came to his knowledge in 1882. He was able to call some heavyweight witnesses – Major James Walker, long-time Chairman of the Midland Association of Flint Glass Manufacturers, Walter Packwood, a former Central Secretary of the FGMFS, and Joseph Leicester, another leading figure in the Union and briefly MP for West Ham. They testified that the equipment was a great improvement on previous processes, and a novelty in the trade when it was first patented in 1876. Richardson maintained that he was the original inventor. Two of his workmen, Blood and Woolley, gave evidence that they had visited the defendants' works and bought glass there, made with the same apparatus that had been patented. (It is not apparent which of the Woolley family members this was, but "Blood" was very likely the venerable-bearded Carpenter, William Blood (see Chapter 5 below), who may have been responsible for constructing the apparatus}.

Castry and Gee defended their position vigorously, maintaining that the apparatus was no novelty and that they were already using it in 1876 when Richardson applied for his patent. As well as their own employees, they also called as witnesses the proprietor and several workers of Bolton's Glassworks in Warrington to say that their firm had been using similar equipment from the early 1870's.

Richardson made no better impression on the High Court Judge than he had on the Sudbury magistrates back in 1881. M'Lord's comments were hostile to the plaintiff from the start and he eventually gave judgement for the defendants "with costs on the higher scale."

• FGMFS officers continued to selflessly visit the Dove Valley. Between May 1888 and February 1889, a number of Tutbury District members were recompensed by their Union on three occasions - firstly for *"resisting a rise in numbers"* (that is, the number of articles required that had to be blown per "turn", i.e., shift); secondly *"through loss of work, three moves"*; and thirdly for having *"to leave off work through bad metal, the employer refusing to give them another pattern."* And in the autumn of 1889: *"We had an important case in Tutbury, which was a sliding scale of wages. We have met with many anomalies in our time, but this was an outrage on common sense. The CS and one of the Executive visited the district as requested and we are glad to say put an end to this system."*

• At the time of the 1891 Census 103 local inhabitants can be identified as employed in the glass industry, including 17 residing in Hatton and Scropton. John T H Richardson was living in Scropton Lane, a Flint Glass Manufacturer. No indication is given on this Census of the number of his employees, though it is probable that the reduction since 1881 in the total number employed in the locality had taken place at the RCGW. He had been joined in the management of the business by his elder son Frederick John, now aged 27, a Glass

Works Manager. His other children were not at home, but the domestic staff had increased to two. His younger son, Thomas Haden Richardson aged 25, was a visitor to Reddish Hall south of Manchester and home of Donald MacPherson, a Colour and Varnish Manufacturer; Thomas gave his occupation as Glass Manufacturer.

* * * * *

The Royal Castle Glass Works 1891-1901: Decline and Fall

• The years after 1891 continued to see Richardson and his Glass Blowers in regular confrontation. The underlying cause was the severe depression that the glass trade, along with most other manufacturing sectors, suffered through this period, intensified by cheap foreign competition. Glass manufacturers like Richardson fought to survive as best they could, but in their view were not helped by the intransigence of the powerful Glass Blowers' Union in protecting their craft practices and wage structures.

- In early 1893 the FGMM reported: *"A firm at Tutbury (Messrs Richardsons) have stopped work, ostensibly to reduce their stock, this of course may be the sole reason for the stoppage but at the same time the furnace is undergoing repairs or alterations, and according to the notices received by the men I should think alterations of the furnace have something to do with the stoppage..."* On this occasion, they did restart work quickly.

- But by summer of that year: *"Tutbury seems to be getting worse from one quarter to another, and the coal question seems to be adding to their difficulties."* (There was a national lock-out in the Coal Industry in 1893, which severely curtailed supplies of fuel to manufacturing industries).

47

- In early 1894, the Union's Central Committee reported: *"We have had one or two disputes; one at Tutbury, where a whole factory of men are out on the principle of a week's wage or a week's work. The men only worked seven turns in four weeks, and the employer would not pay them their wages. The CS and one of the representatives went to see the employer, but he would not pay, so the men asked permission to leave and they have been out some weeks... The men were completely starved out, and it is the first time in my experience to see men rejoice when we gave them permission to give in their notices. I have been able to get a few in work, and we have only six left."* The FGMM unemployment register identifies the men affected, who are clearly the regular RCGW contingent: Ben Bell, John Woolley, James Woolley, George Woolley, Harry Woolley, William Harding, John Pye, Edward Bennett, J Bridges, H Stanley, W Kenyon, F Parrish, L Press and F Johnson. They were off for a fortnight in the middle of January, returned to work for two weeks, and were then permanently off from 10th February. By April four of the men had been sent to London and one to Glasgow. The remainder stayed at home drawing unemployment pay which reduced over the course of the year from thirteen to six shillings per week. In April Richardson was trying to recruit non-Union labour, advertising in the Manchester Courier and Lancashire General Advertiser: *"Flint Glass Trade. Wanted, Men for Tumblers and Wine Chairs. Address to Mr Richardson, Tutbury."* But the Union reported that the dispute was resolved "satisfactorily" by October 1894, though no further details are given, and the local men returned to work.

- 1895 appears to have been free of major disputes, but by May 1896 the Hatton men were drawing unemployment pay again. The background to this is unknown, but it is likely that the RCGW was shut down as the number of contributing Union members in the Tutbury District dropped from twenty-eight to only sixteen (which would be the Ludgate Street workforce). Benjamin Bell was re-directed by the

Union to work in St Helens and then to Warrington, where he was joined by eight colleagues; three others, including John and Harry Woolley, went to Stourbridge.

• On 9th and 17th October 1896, the Derbyshire Advertiser & Journal carried a Notice on its front page by auctioneers Graham and Darley for a sale by auction to be held on 21st October at the Castle Hotel, near Tutbury Station. The main lot was described as a freehold property known as the Royal Castle Glassworks, for many years in the occupation of Mr JTH Richardson. Included was a parcel of turf land eligible for building purposes, fronting the Hatton-Tutbury main road.

Lot 2 was a Standard Life Policy of Assurance for £1,000 upon the life of a "gentleman now aged 61 years", taken out in 1873 and with accrued bonuses of £320. Richardson, born in January 1835, was 61 years old, and the policy was surely on him.

The ownership of the Scropton Lane property has been unclear until this point – both during Sivewright's start-up and Richardson's operation of the glassworks. Though the Seller of the freehold is not identified in the auction Notice, the juxtaposition of the life policy sale indicates that it was Richardson himself.

He must have been at the end of his tether. His wife was dying, and the business and financial pressures on him were relentless. Putting both his factory premises and a personal insurance policy up for public sale must have been deeply humiliating. The results of the auction are not known, but it is likely that the freehold found a buyer in James Eadie, a leading Burton Brewer – see Chapter 5 below.

• The following year Richardson managed to get the factory up to speed again, as the CS reported in October 1897: *"It is cheering and stimulating to report a decided improvement in trade. We have had three new furnaces started during the quarter – one in Birmingham, one in Stourbridge, and one in Tutbury – independent of a large demand for men. I hope the good ending of a trying year may continue, and wish all the above firms a hearty success".* The CS visited Tutbury *"re the starting of a new place"*, and he, Benjamin Bell and John Woolley met with Richardson *"re the Wages Question"*. The Union's Executive Committee minutes at the time recorded: *"Tutbury Case: Resolved that we agree to give the place another trial."*

This is yet another example of the "love-hate" relationship that prevailed between the FGMFS and Richardson across the years - recurrent and often bitter disagreements, strikes and closures, punctuated by reconciliations and a renewed joint willingness to keep the RCGW afloat. The relationship appears to be almost unique in the industry, possibly explained by Richardson's origins in the Stourbridge glass "aristocracy", the Union's recognition of the depressed trading context in which he was trying to survive, and even a soft spot amongst the FGMFS bigwigs for the quirky, isolated Tutbury/Hatton outpost of the industry.

• Richardson's wife Sarah had died on 11th November 1896 aged 68 and was buried in Tutbury. Shortly after her mother's death, their only daughter Katie was married on 8th May 1897 to Joseph Preston Ward at St Mary's, Marston-on-Dove. The Burton Chronicle reported that the wedding was a quiet one because of the recent family bereavement. Much of the report is given over to a lengthy list of the wedding presents and their donors. The bride's present to the groom was a signet ring, but the groom responded more unconventionally with the gift to Katie of a bicycle. They left for their honeymoon in North Wales on the 2.25 pm train from Tutbury Station "saluted by a volley of fog signals". They later moved to Builth Wells in mid-Wales, where her husband was involved in the management of a brewery.

Katie had one child, a daughter Muriel Ward, who married in turn but had no children of her own.

And so, within six months, the Richardson household in Scropton Lane became a purely male affair. It is tempting to mark the terminal decline in the family's star from this time.

• One great day was still to come however. On 23rd August 1899 the Hull Daily Mail (!) reported in its "Social Record" that *"The Duchess of York yesterday visited Tutbury, Burton-on-Trent, and went to the Royal Castle Glass Works, at Hatton, and subsequently to the Works of the Photo Decorative Tile Company."* The Manchester Courier added that the Duke and Duchess were staying with the Honourable SJ and Lady Catherine Coke at nearby Longford Hall at the time. The Duchess, later Queen Mary to George V, was very much the Princess Diana of her day.

Understandably, the local press made quite a splash of the visit, and the full report from the Burton Chronicle is transcribed in Appendix B. The article provides a detailed description of the various factory departments, and confirms that the RCGW was a typical producer of hand-blown tableware using a range of decorating processes:

"The Royal party were received by Mr J T H Richardson, and at the Glass Works the mixing room was first visited, samples of the ingredients used in making the staple article being inspected with much interest by her Royal Highness. A move was then made to the glass house, where the men were engaged in making wine glasses, glass jugs, and shades. At the Duchess's request a beautiful flower vase was manufactured in her presence, to be sent to her at York House, as a souvenir of her visit. She expressed great surprise at the expeditious and workmanlike manner in which the molten glass was manipulated, particularly ornaments such as swans, Jacob's Ladders

and miniature Wellington boots, etc. After spending half-an-hour in the glass house the party repaired to the annealing ovens, where the glass is allowed to gradually cool. The cutting shop was next visited, the various processes the glass has to go through, including roughing, smoothing and polishing, being witnessed with great delight. Then the party went to the stoppering room, where decanters are fitted with stoppers, and afterwards saw the sand blast process of decorating jugs, bottles, tumblers, etc. The etching, printing and engraving rooms were in turn inspected, and at the latter place the Duchess herself decorated a wine glass with a circle border, and desired that it should be forwarded on to her. The large, clean, well-lighted show rooms next received attention. And in the course of her perambulations her Royal Highness particularly admired some samples of wine glasses of the Queen Anne pattern, and claret jugs ornamented with the Prince of Wales' feathers, and hunting scenes, and expressed great astonishment at the sight of a glass flower vase, 10ft high, which had been made on the premises."

The Duchess's encounter with the Glass Blowers was particularly well-remembered locally: *"One of the men made with lightening rapidity a small model of a pig, whereupon her Royal Highness humorously remarked that that was not the kind of animal described in the song "When the pigs begin to fly." "Oh! Your Royal Highness," said the man, "we can soon get over that difficulty," and almost before one could say "Jack Robinson" the pig was adorned with a pair of wings, the incident provoking much laughter, in which the Duchess heartily joined, and requested that it should be despatched with numerous other articles to York House."*

Wilfred Woolley, writing to Mr WH Bennett in 1973, added some names to this incident: *"There was quite a party of them... However, during their stay, as they were watching, one of the old glassmakers approached the party with a piece of metal on his blowing iron and said to one of the ladies "Have a blow through this, Mrs York." The man's name was Timmins. My father was working there at the time, and as they gathered round his chair to watch him at work, he made them a number of glass novelties. Then someone made a joke about the old saying that "Pigs might fly". When my father heard this he at once made a pig with wings which caused more merriment."* William Timmins probably dined (or drank) out on his moment of fame for the rest of his life. Even when his death was briefly reported by the Nottingham Daily Post in September 1932, it was under the heading "The Queen's Glass Pig" with another version of events: *"The death at Tutbury of William Timmins, retired glassblower recalls the visit of Queen Mary to Tutbury glassworks over 30 years ago. At the request of the Duchess of York, as she then was, Timmins made her a glass swan, and workmates fashioned a glass pig, embellishing it with glass wings. Timmins used to relate how the duchess merrily remarked as she accepted the souvenir, "When the pigs begin to fly, won't the pork be rather high?"*

Mr Woolley adds some confusion as well: *"Now about the Royal visit. There is no doubt about it taking place, but it was at the top shop, not the bottom shop."* There is a pencil note on his letter by Mr Bennett: *"No - definitely Castle Glass"*, and the press coverage makes clear that the 1899 visit was to the "Bottom Shop". The reporting is also further evidence that the Castle Glass Works "Royal" designation pre-dates this visit and did not arise as a consequence of it.

• The following splendid photograph has survived, and has been previously attributed as *"A group of managers and workers at the Royal Castle Glassworks c.1900-1910"*. The location appears to be correct but, as will be seen below, the RCGW ran into difficulties and probably closed in 1900, and the photo more likely dates from the mid to late 1890's. The photograph shows the aftermath of the arduous task of "pot-setting" - the end-of-week process in which the containers used to hold the raw materials for firing are changed.

Figure 13 – Let me show you how the other half lives...

Fifteen glassblowers, a gentleman and a young lady stand around the old pot which has been removed, red-hot, from the furnace into the yard using an elongated trolley. The faces of the blowers are etched with the sweat and grime of the process.

No authenticated photographs of JTH Richardson have yet come to light, and it would be very satisfying to identify the gentleman and young lady as Richardson and perhaps his daughter Katie. However, in the opinion of a Victorian fashion expert, the girl's clothes and appearance (short skirt and pigtails) indicate that she is no more than a teenager, which would imply a mid to late 1880's date if it was Katie, who was born in 1868. But as explained below, a number of the workmen can be identified with confidence against later photographs, and their ages seem to preclude any date for this picture before the mid 1890's. In fact, the gentleman can be identified with reasonable certainty as Richardson's son Tom, who is named in a Tutbury Cricket Club photograph of 1911:

Figure 14 Tom Richardson c1895?   Figure 15 Tom Richardson 1911

Was exposure to the fiery hell of the Glass House an unusual Saturday morning thrill for his young friend in her pristine white blouse? She remains unidentified.

It has to be said that everyone appears reasonably relaxed and comfortable with each other, unlike many of the severely posed photographs of the period - this despite the frequently acrimonious employer/employee relations at the RCGW in those years. (Standing behind the young lady appears to be none other than John Woolley.)

A first guide to the dating of the picture is the distinctive thin face of the second man on the left. He is unmistakably the George Woolley identified on a 1910 photograph of an RCGW works outing (see Chapter 4). By 1910 he was a rather elderly looking fifty-year-old, certainly a good ten years or more in age than the man on this earlier photo. George also acts as a link back to the 1882-85 dispute with the Union, where he figured at both the outset and the resolution of the conflict, and in a lighter vein further back to the 1877 cricket match.

The burly figure sixth from the left can also be identified with some confidence as the William Nicklin aged 46 on the 1910 picture, with again probably more than a ten-year age difference between the two images. The man fourth from the left holding a blowing iron is fairly certainly Harry McGuiness, custodian of the hunting horn in 1910 photograph, when he was aged 44. Both Nicklin and McGuiness appear to be at least in their late twenties in the earlier photograph, if not more, which implies a mid-1890's date at the earliest (thus ruling out Katie Richardson as the young lady).

The window of the building does not fit with those visible on the 1879 engraving of the Works, but pots would most likely have been taken out to the back of the Glass House which is not seen on the engraving.

A second pot-setting photograph survives with largely the same men, taken in the RCGW yard at around the same time. George Woolley and Nicklin both appear on this, as does Michael Molloy who also appears on the 1910 photo in older age. Molloy was the Tutbury District FGMFS President across the period 1883-86 when the long-running dispute took place, working himself at the Tutbury Glassworks. If, by the 1890's, he had moved to the Hatton Glassworks, it confirms that there was indeed an element of letting bygones be bygones in the RCGW worker/employer relationship in the later years.

Figure 16 – Another hard morning's pot-setting in the 1890s

• On the 1901 Census, JTH Richardson was living in Scropton Road, aged 66 and widowed, still describing himself as a Flint Glass Manufacturer. His sons were with him, Frederick aged 37 and Thomas aged 35, both Glass Works Managers. There was no-one else in the house.

However, there are convincing indications that the Hatton Glassworks had effectively ceased production by 1900. This is despite the three Richardsons' description of their occupation in 1901; and the fact that Kelly's Post Office Directories for 1900 and 1904 continued to list JTH Richardson as a Flint Glass Manufacturer with his address at the Castle Glassworks. In evidence of the closure, the combined workforce employed in the glass industry and living in Tutbury and

Hatton in 1901 had fallen to just 57 from its 1891 level of 103. There are no indications that the Tutbury factory was closed at this time and therefore the reduction stems most likely from a shutdown of the Hatton Works. Besides the Richardsons, only four other Glassworkers were living in Hatton.

But, as usual, the most conclusive evidence is found in the FGMFS unemployment records. Eight RCGW Blowers were out of work for three weeks from the end of July 1899, and from 28th November they were out again. Five non-local men also moved to Stourbridge at that time. Together they probably formed the entirety of the Hatton Blowing Shop. This time the closure was permanent and Richardson's Phoenix, which had risen so many times before from the ashes, finally faded away.

There is no narrative reference in the Union records to the demise of the RCGW, nor has any newspaper comment been found as yet – the Works, as a functioning production unit, just quietly disappeared from the scene. A widespread depression in the Glass Tableware trade continued into the 1900's, culminating in a major national Lock-out in 1902, hardly the time to try and revive the business. The eight local men out of work were the Woolleys, John, Henry and Tom, Benjamin Bell, John Donkin, William Timmins, John Pye and John Bridges, surviving on the diminishing scale of unemployment pay from the Union. Henry Woolley and John Donkin transferred to Edinburgh a year later. John Woolley found a position at Ludgate Street before later going to Stourbridge. Benjamin Bell retired and was able to draw his Union pension from the end of 1901. Thomas Woolley died in October 1902. Timmins, Pye and Bridges were still unemployed in late 1902. The local Union membership was almost halved, falling from thirty-one contributing members in 1899 to seventeen in the following years, leaving they District in permanent financial deficit.

Further anecdotal evidence of the closure also comes from Mr Wilfred Woolley, born in 1887, and writing in his 1973 letter referred to above: *"Things were not too good in the trade at that time at the bottom shop, and my father (and no doubt the other men too) worked for weeks with no pay, to try to keep the shop going. All they got was promises of money to come. However, a chair became vacant at the top shop and my father went there. Later on, he went to Stourbridge."* It is evident in 1900, as at many other times, that a top-class Blower was almost always able to find work, particularly if he was prepared to travel. But Cutters and less skilled Blowers found it more difficult. Examples are James Archer who was a Glass Cutter on both the 1891 and 1911 Censuses, but in the bad times of 1901 was a Gardener's Labourer. Similarly, John Bentley, a Glassmaker's Apprentice in 1891, was working as a Loader at the Fauld Mine in 1901, and then found his way back into the industry as a Glass Mixer in 1911.

* * * * *

Final days of the Richardson Family

• It may be that in the years after 1900 some form of operation was maintained at the RCGW for a while, on a very reduced level, perhaps not involving manufacture but just the merchanting of glassware - mirroring, ironically, Sivewright's efforts at making a living after his bankruptcy. For example, in September 1908 the Derby Telegraph reported that two youths were found guilty at Sudbury Petty Sessions of stealing six cut glass water bottles, one stopper and one ring tray from a *"warehouse at Hatton, property of Mr J T H Richardson."*

More anecdotal evidence comes from local historian Mr Aubrey Bailey: *"Around 1900, depression in the glass industry caused a temporary closure of the Hatton works, but further evidence shows that manufacture was revived in 1902 as the decanter and wines you see on the screen were given to my own mother and father who were* married in April that year, as a wedding present by Mr Thomas Richardson who, with his brother Frederick, assisted in the management of the Company acquired by their father, Thomas Haden Richardson." Mr Bailey, uncharacteristically, may be wrong about a 1902 revival. By contrast, Mr WH Bennett, managing director of Trent Valley Glassworks, wrote: "A trade slump in 1900 caused the works to close down and as far as is known, it did not re-open until around 1910." So it may well be that the wedding present came from warehouse stock rather than current production.

• Aubrey Bailey's note is one of the few brief references to the roles of the two sons in the business. It was noted earlier that Thomas Richardson witnessed the Apprentice Indenture of Harry Woolley in 1884 - Thomas was eighteen at the time, and it appears that he and probably his elder brother Frederick were by then already supporting their father in the family firm in those difficult times. Their responsibility, if any, in the decline of the firm is not known. It would be easy to speculate about an autocratic father holding back the sons' talents by refusing to let go of the reins, or equally about the disappointment of an old man in the boys' inability to live up to their talented Richardson pedigree and keep the business going. They certainly would have enjoyed a fairly "gilded youth", and the temptations of the rugby and cricket fields would have been a ready distraction from the burdens of running a struggling factory.

It is also sobering to find the 1900 closure following so closely on the heels of the spectacular day of the Royal visit a year before. How many cracks was Richardson having to paper over as he guided his distinguished visitors around the Works?

It does seem however that the three men at least avoided bankruptcy, as no insolvency proceedings have been found in the London Gazette. This is slightly surprising as it was an unincorporated business, not a limited company, with the partners therefore personally liable for debts. Whether Wilfred Woolley's father and other workers ever got their back pay is not known, but the Richardsons must have found a way to satisfy their other creditors.

• As well as his probable glass merchanting, Richardson senior dabbled elsewhere to secure an income. Somewhat bizarrely, according to a Notice in the Derby Daily Telegraph, he was appointed part-time Engineer by Repton Rural District Council to oversee the tendering process for new sewerage infrastructure in Hatton in October 1904, operating from "his office near Tutbury Station". Additionally, there is conflicting evidence about the extent of Richardson's involvement with the Photo Decorated Tile Works, an innovative venture which operated on the site adjoining the RCGW, and was also visited by the 1899 Royal party. The story of that business is told in Appendix C.

• One wonders how the ageing Richardson looked on the resurrection in 1910 of his disused works by the brash George Harry Corbett. Perhaps with the same mixed feelings that Sivewright may have had forty years earlier, when Richardson himself had been the bright young saviour of glassmaking in Hatton.

• On the 1911 Census John Thomas Haden Richardson, a retired Flint Glass Manufacturer, was living in a five-roomed dwelling referred to as "The Glassworks, Hatton". With him was his son, Thomas, aged 46 and unmarried, an Insurance Agent. The preceding and following houses on the Census had Scropton Road addresses, though the local Enumerator unhelpfully omitted to include house numbers or names on the Return Sheets for Scropton Lane over the decades.

There is a note added to the 1955 recollections of Frank Pegg: *"Richardsons ejected in 1913 from his [sic] living accommodation on the works."* This would appear to confirm that the Richardson house was actually on the RCGW site. Frustratingly no residential building has yet been identified in photographs, maps or documents or the recollection of Harry Shaw, that could feasibly have been the home over the years of the once well-to-do entrepreneur and his wife and children - surely not the humble dwelling suggested as the possible residence occupied by Mr and Mrs Wardle in 1871?

Opposite the site on the other side of Scropton Lane, there still stands today "Stanley House", a comfortable detached dwelling, which would certainly have befitted the factory owner both as regards location and status. And it was at Stanley House that his son Frederick Richardson was living many years later when he died in 1938 (see below). There is also a Cricket Club reference to the brothers "of Stanley House", possibly dated to 1891. It is tempting to suppose that Stanley House was in fact the Richardson family home across the years before 1911. It has an 1862 building stone. Is it a coincidence that Sivewright's first Glassworks was built about 1863? Mr Shaw believes that they may have been built together, and though we know that Sivewright was living in High Street, Tutbury in both 1861 and 1871, that is not to say he wasn't in Hatton between 1863 and 1868. But Frank Pegg's note and the Census "Glassworks" address contradict this, and imply that the Richardsons moved from the factory site to Stanley House in 1913 or later. A mystery yet to be resolved…

It will be seen in Chapter 5 that 1913 was a turbulent time at the RCGW, with an acrimonious change of control from George Harry Corbett to Stanley Noel Jenkinson. Richardson's continued tenure of a house on the site could easily have been a casualty of the events of that time. He was then aged 78, within a year of his death, and it must have been a distressing conclusion to his long and once successful association with the RCGW.

John Thomas Haden Richardson died on 12th January 1914 and was buried three days later alongside his wife, in a fine spot on the bank outside the celebrated west door of St Mary's Priory Church, Tutbury.

Figure 17 - The Richardson grave

The plain grave is now sadly neglected - understandably so, as it is many years since the last of Richardson's descendants were alive to tend it. But, a century after his death, his life has at least been recalled in these pages. As well as Richardson, the gravestone records his wife who had died eighteen years earlier, and also a Jonathon

Richardson who had died in 1867 aged 21. This was his younger brother, who was in Tutbury, away from his Stourbridge home, when he died, but whether working at the Tutbury factory or just on a family visit is not at present known.

A number of local newspapers reported on Richardson's passing. The Uttoxeter Advertiser called it the *"Death of a Hatton Worthy"*, saying that *"The Tutbury area, and Hatton in particular, has lost one of its best-known and most respected inhabitants in the person of Mr J T H Richardson."* It went on to recount his arrival in 1863 as Managing Partner of the Tutbury Glass Company followed by his establishment of the Works in Hatton in 1871. His many improvements in the manufacture of glass were referred to, his several public offices and, of course, the Royal visit to the RCGW. It recalled that *"during the heyday of his business prosperity [he] traveled largely [sic] in connection with its development."* Richardson's later decline in fortune must have been a fairly public and painful spectacle, but the obituary's emphasis on his finer days is both poignant and appropriate.

• Richardson's son, Thomas Haden Richardson, stayed on in the district and his death was registered in the Burton-on-Trent District in 1923 aged 58 (only a year after knocking his half century against Denstone on the Plaster Mill cricket ground). Neither he nor his father appears to have left a will.

• In 1911 the second son Frederick Richardson, aged 47 and also unmarried, was living alone in two rooms in Manchester, describing himself as a Political Agent for a Conservative Association and "late Flint Glass Manufacturer". At some point he returned to the local area. Interestingly, in 1932, he was one of the leading non-family mourners at the funeral of John Woolley, who had stuck with the Richardsons in the 1880's. Frederick Richardson of Stanley House,

Scropton Lane died in August 1939 at the General Infirmary in Burton, his estate just £148 - an undistinguished end to this line of the illustrious Richardsons of Stourbridge.

Nevertheless, John Thomas Haden Richardson's years at the helm of the Royal Castle Glass Works can be looked on as one of the two successful eras of glassmaking in Hatton, if only as regards longevity. (The second was that of Trent Valley Glassworks from 1947 to 1983). From the early 1870's to the late 1890's, the business was commercially active, recruited skilled craftsmen, developed substantial premises, and even attracted royal patronage. This was at a time when trading conditions in the industry were, more often than not, severely depressed, and when the rival Tutbury Glassworks seemed moribund. Richardson must have possessed a capable range of business skills and knowledge of the glass trade to achieve this. However, the continuous disputes with his men and their Union in the 1880/90's and the eventual closure of the business at the turn of the century leave us with a more nuanced picture of his career and character.

* * * * *

4.   1905-1910   The Anchor & Cross Bottle Works

Five years after the demise of Richardson's Royal Castle Glass Works, a group of London investors established a new "model" factory for the automatic production of glass bottles and jars on a second site in Scropton Lane. The origins, aims and launch of the business can best be described by quoting a Burton Mail report of Wednesday 4th October 1905:

"NEW ERA IN BOTTLE MAKING
MODEL WORKS OPENED AT TUTBURY
BLOWING GIVES WAY TO MACHINERY
Tutbury near Burton-on-Trent has suffered for so many years under the effects of depression in the glass trade that the ceremony of starting the fires in the new bottle works which was duly observed this (Wednesday) morning should cause the liveliest satisfaction. The new works which have been built by the Trades Progress Company Limited for the Anchor & Cross Bottle Works Syndicate Limited, London, on land adjacent to the company's own site by Scropton Road, contain the first complete plant of its kind in Europe, the aim of the engineers having been to reduce the cost of production in every process involved in the bottle-making industry as compared with existing methods.

For instance, although employment will be found for some 70 or 80 operatives - men, youths and girls - with the exception of two or three men all the employees will be unskilled workers. Generally in bottle works the material is handled several times by skilled and highly paid workers in the course of manufacture, but the new plant at Tutbury has been so designed and arranged that all unnecessary re-handling of the material is obviated, the sand and other raw materials entering the works by a railway siding at one end and the finished ware being loaded into railway trucks at the other, the movement of the materials through the works thus being a continuous operation in one direction.

The new buildings, which have been erected during the course of the summer, include the glass house (built of brick and steel) and warehouse of brick with wood superstructure, all covered with corrugated metal. Special provision has been made for ventilation, so that the workmen will be able to work without feeling the extreme heat. The plant consists of a continuous regenerative tank furnace, designed to produce a quality of glass unequalled in such a furnace in Europe, viz., white flint glass. With the furnace is the necessary gas producing plant, and a continuous annealing furnace for the tempering of ware.

The production of bottles is wholly a machine operation, the ware being produced at a great gain of speed over hand methods, while a marked advance is likewise noted in the quality of the ware. These machines are of two kinds - (1) for the manufacture of all kinds of jars and open-mouthed wares and (2) for the manufacture of various forms of narrow-necked bottles. The motive power for operating the machinery is all supplied by a gas engine, which drives the cooling fans, the air compressing plant, water pumps, batch elevators, etc.

A representative of this journal has made a tour of the new works,, under the genial chaperonage of Mr Vincent J. MacIntyre, the Manager of the Trades Progress Company Limited."

[There then follows a lengthy description of the "continuous regenerative tank furnace", which we will spare the reader.]

"The kindling of the fires is an event of no small moment in the history of a glass works for, given ordinary good luck, they are not allowed to

cool down for months, and perhaps for a year at a time. Hence the ceremony enacted this morning by Miss Short, daughter of the chairman of the Anchor and Cross Bottle Works Syndicate, although practically a private function, was regarded with a lot of interest in Tutbury. The directors assembled together with their friends, and entertained the workmen who have been engaged in the construction of the works, to lunch.

In the presence of the directors, officials and workpeople, Miss Short gracefully carried out the ceremony this afternoon of lighting the fires. Armed with a long flaming torch, she kindled the various fires, with the exception of the furnaces which require a few days drying. The company included Mr W.H. Short (chairman of the company), Col. Benson and Mr L.P. Montefiore (directors), Mr Liardet (who is to be the general manager of the works), Mr Arthur Tilliard (solicitor to the company), Mr Knight, Mr Lamont (engineer and works manager), Mr Vincent MacIntyre and Mr MacIntyre Snr., Mrs and Miss Short, Mrs Liardet, and Miss Kenworthy.

After the new works had been inspected, the company, together with the workmen, numbering about 50, who have been engaged in the erection of the works and the plant, sat down to a capital lunch, after which the chairman (Mr Short) proposed "Success to the new undertaking". More than two years ago, he said, the idea of starting a small works to demonstrate in this country the making of bottles by machine process, and particularly the making of bottles which could be filled and emptied, but never refilled, was brought to his notice and that of his colleagues by Mr MacIntyre and Mr Liardet. It took him by surprise, and filled him with an immense amount of enthusiasm. They tried and tried to raise sufficient money to start the works, and had arrived at the stage they had witnessed. He had not the slightest doubt but that they had lighted a fire in Tutbury that would keep burning for many years (Applause). They trusted it was going to burn *for the success not only of those who had found the means of lighting the fires, but all those who were going to assist in working it. He had every confidence in Mr MacIntyre as their consulting engineer, Mr Lamont as the works manager, Mr Liardet and his (the speaker's) son, who was going to look after the office details. He concluded by wishing all success, and hoping all engaged in working the plant would be loyal. (Applause).*

Col. Benson, on behalf of the directors, then placed a handsome diamond and opal ring upon Miss Short's finger, expressing the hope that the fires she had lighted would never go out, and that the works would meet with every success. Miss Short returned thanks for the gift, reiterating Col. Benson's good wishes for the success of the works.

Mr Tilliard proposed the health of Mr MacIntyre, who had designed and built the works. He (the speaker) had known and experienced the difficulty of starting the works, and he hoped there would come success not only to those who had promoted the company, but also to those who would work in it, and especially in this connection to Mr Macintyre. (Applause, and musical honours).

Mr MacIntyre, in reply, referred to the responsibilities and difficulties besetting anyone in attempting to establish a new method in bottle-making. He hoped that the fire Miss Short had started would be a fire of prosperity, heralding a revolution in the glass trade. The English glass industry had fallen upon evil days, but they hoped the new works would bring success to those gentlemen who had the courage to invest their capital in an untried enterprise. He had visited glass works in all the countries of Europe and America, and knew the conditions that prevailed. The people who worked at those works would work under conditions far better than those found in the trade generally. (Loud applause). If they would loyally co-operate with the managers, they would get a better return for their services than at any other glassworks in the country. Those machines did not require skilled labour. The methods of bottle making of 50 years ago did not fill the bill at the present time; it was necessary to make them cheaply, so that they could get their beer and whisky at reasonable prices. He emphasized, in conclusion, that machine production increased the demand for labour, and was the secret of the country's commercial progress. (Applause).

Mr Liardet, in response to his health, proposed by Mr Montefiore, said that until recently bottles were still made as they were in the days of Pharaoh, but Mr MacIntyre had given them a new method by which they did not blow down pipes. (Laughter and applause). Other complimentary toasts followed, and the company dispersed after hearty cheering for the success of the venture."

• Companies House records provide more detail on the origins of the enterprise. The Anchor & Cross Bottle Works Syndicate Ltd was incorporated in June 1904 with an initial authorised share capital of £6,500, its principal objective to carry on the business of glass manufacturers and to enter into an agreement with the Liardet Non-Refillable Bottle Company and Arthur Charles Cavendish Liardet. The initial subscriber shareholders were:

Colonel Starling Benson, J.P.; Walter Short, a Chartered Accountant; Victor Martin, a Stockbroker; Robert Baker, an Accountant's Clerk; Arthur Tilliard, a Solicitor; John Madden, a Barrister; and
Charles D'Oyley Hutchins, an Electrical Engineer.

The company issued a share prospectus, inviting the public to subscribe for shares. This first financing attempt did not get off the ground and Walter Short later informed Companies House that "the company did not go to allotment and has never carried on business."

It was finally dissolved in 1908. A second company "The New Anchor & Cross Bottle Works Syndicate Ltd" was incorporated in March 1905, with an almost identical Memorandum and Articles and issued an almost identical Prospectus. Copies are held by Tutbury Museum (ref GL403). It appears that this time funds were successfully raised, £1,759 in ordinary share capital from some twenty-five private investors in London and the Home Counties together with the three directors. 2,500 "Founders" Shares were issued to the company promoters as consideration for their time and expenses in launching the enterprise and a £2,000 debenture loan was also taken out. The company entered into the agreement with Arthur Liardet. The directors of the new company were Colonel Benson, Walter Short and Louis Philip Montefiore, Gentleman, which ties in with those described at the inaugural lunch.

In the following year a further £1,755 debenture loan was raised and £2,950 new share capital was issued, of which £1,850 came from John Sinclair Hamilton, a Book Publisher from Woking, who had taken up £100 of the initial share offering. Hamilton was appointed a director in November 1906.

These gentlemen were just financiers, however. From the opening ceremony report, it is clear that the technical input came from Liardet, Lamont and more particularly MacIntyre's Trades Progress Company. And although he was never a director or employee of the Anchor & Cross, Victor McIntyre as Consulting Engineer to the company should probably be looked on as the key provider of enterprise and ingenuity that led to the establishment of a Bottle Works in Hatton. Companies House information on The Trades Progress Company Ltd is detailed in Appendix D.

• Mr Wilfred Woolley's 1973 recollections give a picture of the glass operation's progress from a shop floor perspective:

"I was born in the year 1887 and started work as a presser at the Anchor & Cross Bottleworks when I was 18 years old. These works had only recently started and they were having a bit of trouble, chiefly with the metal, and the machines were very difficult to work if the metal was not just right. Mr Lamont, the manager, walked about with a very worried look on his face. However, things were gradually put right and we were on the way to a pretty good production. There were six machines on the shop floor, all press & blow, and worked by compressed air. The metal was dropped into the parison mould by the gatherer, the presser pushed a lever and down came the plunger with a bang; the plunger went back and the parison shape was transferred to the blow mould; two seconds of compressed air and the completed jar was taken out of the blower. The larger machines were a bit different, the 1lb and 2lb jam jars were fixed to a turntable and, after pressing, the parison shape was moved on to the first blow mould and there blown and taken out by the blower. This carried on continuously. I was on a smaller machine making 2oz Vaseline jars and had to do the lot myself, a pair of shoes in one hand and a stick in the other for 10 hours per day with one half hour break. By this time, we were doing very well and we were on piecework, but the money was low. I was paid three and a halfpenny per gross for good ware. The production was all jam jars except a small machine on small screw tops, Vaseline, etc., and the quality was pretty good.

After a short period as the Anchor & Cross, we were evidently taken over by another firm, the British & Foreign Bottle Co, and all the packages had to be labelled with their name and address. Some time later we were again taken over, this time it was the B.G.I. (British Glass Industries) and finally we were taken by Canning Town Glass and that is where they are now. After about two years working (as near as I can recall) Mr Lamont disappeared and the Langwells, Wilfred and Ted, came to manage the place and remained to the end. All the production had to go to London by the railway and as the transport became more and more of a burden our management contacted the Railway people with a suggestion for lower charges, but the Railway would not agree, and the whole factory and all the workers moved to Queenborough, where the transport was by sailing barge and much cheaper."

• Mr Woolley does not mention one particularly eventful day for the furnace men. Again, a local newspaper reported the incident vividly, this time the Derby Daily Telegraph on 5th September 1908:

*"**EXCITING SCENE AT TUTBURY GLASS WORKS. Blast Furnace Collapses. A STREAM OF MOLTEN GLASS.** Tutbury Glass Works [sic] were this (Saturday) morning the scene of a most exciting incident and fire. At about 9 o'clock, while work was in full progress, without warning of any kind one of the blast furnaces collapsed, and about 32 tons of red-hot glass fell out. The glass which at this heat is liquid, poured forth in a strong, steady stream. Workmen from all parts of the premises ran to the assistance of the three men in charge of the furnace. The party succeeded in hastily throwing up a brick wall, but the stream slowly moved forward on to the rooms in which chemicals were stored, swamping barrels of arsenic and setting fire to a number of packing cases.*

A big blaze seemed inevitable, as the flames were soon communicated to the woodwork of the building itself. The fire appliances on the premises were brought into action, but the men were greatly hampered owing to the intense heat of the molten glass, which covered the floor to the thickness of a foot. However, they were ultimately successful in checking the flow, and on the arrival of the Burton fire brigade, all danger was averted. The estimated damage to the premises is about £50"

This is a fine example of the conflation of the Tutbury and Hatton factories noted in the Introduction. The fire was not at the Tutbury Glass Works of Thomas Webb & Corbett Ltd in Ludgate Street, Tutbury, but at the Anchor & Cross premises in Scropton Lane, Hatton. The Lichfield Mercury two days later clarified the location: *"An outbreak of fire at the new Anchor and Cross Bottle Works, Tutbury on Saturday morning, produced some exciting scenes... Men from the adjoining Tutbury Engineering Works...a lake of glass... damage not at all proportionate to the extraordinary scenes created."*

Figure 18 - Anchor & Cross employees ready for a day out

- The preceding group photograph is of Anchor & Cross employees taken in Hatton some time before the move to Queenborough in Kent in 1910. With most of them in their suits and flowers in their buttonholes, it appears to be the departure for a works outing.

Of the forty-five men pictured, only five are named on the note accompanying the photo. George Acethorpe, grandfather of the donor of the photograph, is first left on the top row. A Blacksmith aged about 37 at the time, he had been employed previously by the Trades Progress Company. When trade there was poor in 1906 he lost his job. He left with a testimonial, of which a copy survives, and found work next door at the Anchor & Cross. (Glassworks frequently employed in-house blacksmiths, as there was a constant need to keep the blowing irons and other metal equipment in good shape). He still appeared with his family in Hatton on the 1911 Census, but moved to the Anchor & Cross's new factory in Kent shortly afterwards.

In the front row centre, fifth from the left, holding his cap, is "Marwood", clearly not a shop floor worker - very likely John William Marwood who was bookkeeper to the Trades Progress Company in 1904, but about whom no other details have yet been established. The young man next but one to the right is "Harry Pye" - he is very probably Henry James Pye, who by 1911 was an Engineer's Machinist aged 22, living in Tutbury. Above him, though his exact position is unclear, is "Tommy Walkman" - unlike Pye, he evidently did move to Kent and in 1911 he was a 59-year-old Pattern Maker at the Queenborough Bottle Works. Finally, "Deville", whose position is also not certain, but probably the bowler hatted man third from the left in the middle row - Deville is a common local name.

If the attribution of this photograph to the Anchor & Cross Bottle Works is correct (there has to be some possibility that it might actually be the adjoining engineering workforce of the Trades Progress Company or Tutbury Engineering), it is interesting that not a single face can be readily tied in with those on the 1890s and 1910 RCGW photos.

When the Anchor & Cross set up in 1905, half of the former glass blowers in the District no longer had jobs in the industry. It is an indication perhaps of how far removed the Anchor & Cross production methods (and probably pay rates) were from the old craft-based methods that so few, if any, of the local skilled glassmakers were tempted to join the new venture.

• The setting to the group photograph is the only picture that has yet come to light of the Anchor & Cross factory and ties in with the brick and corrugated sheeting structure described in the press report at its opening ceremony. The following photograph is of the adjoining works of the Trades Progress Company, builders of the Anchor & Cross works, taken a few years later when it was being operated as the Tutbury Engineering Company.

Figure 19 – The Tutbury Engineering Company (in Hatton...)

The 1922 6" Ordnance Survey map indicates that this photograph is taken from a point adjacent to the railway line looking north east. (The

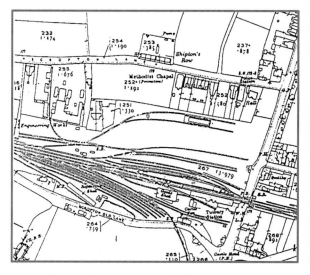

factory name sign would logically be directed at passing railway travellers). Based on the map, the single storey building in the left foreground is in fact separate from the main structure and was part of the former Anchor & Cross premises which are off-picture

Figure 20 – Private Siding into the Bottle Works

to the left. The single-track railway arm into the Anchor & Cross works is shown on the map and can be made out running across the middle of the photograph and between the buildings.

By 1922 the entire site is recorded by the O.S, as an "Engineering Works", and it is fairly certain that after its closure in 1910 the empty Anchor & Cross factory was absorbed into the engineering company's complex. The Tutbury Engineering Company became the Record Engineering Company a few years later.

It continued its involvement as a supplier of equipment to the glassmaking industry. In May 1917 it advertised in the very first edition of the Journal of the Society of Glass Technology (in which Herbert Webb, Chairman of Webb Corbett played a leading role), with special focus on its "Glass Annealing Lehrs, both Belt and Pan Type, Gas Producers...Various Types of Glass Machines, Mechanical Cullet Washer...Moulds Cast and Machined as Required." Five years later the Journal carried the advertisement opposite for their patented Simplex Muffle Lehr, under the name of Record Engineering Co., Ltd. The local glassmaking industry could hardly have provided enough custom to make this business viable. It is rather surprising that the engineering venture was active in this specialised form of product so far away from the major centres of glass production in the West Midlands and North of

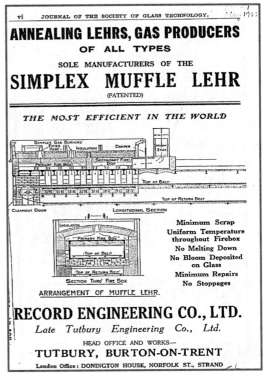

Figure 21 - Record Engineering advertisement

England, which had plenty of "metal-bashers" on their own doorsteps. In 1946 the Record Works site was taken over by Clayton Equipment (later part of International Combustion) and, as a manufacturer of locomotive engines, went through a post-war resurrection and expansion very similar that of Trent Valley Glassworks on the RCGW site next door.

• The operating difficulties described by Wilfred Woolley were reflected in the accounts of the New Anchor & Cross Bottle Works

Syndicate Ltd. A balance sheet dated 31st March 1909 showed accumulated losses since incorporation of £6,650, effectively wiping out the £6,464 capital invested by shareholders. There were liabilities of £9,274 to Debenture Holders and Other Creditors, against assets of £1,679 Plant & Machinery, £751 Stock, £235 Trade Debtors and £6,420 capital expenditure on the Leasehold Premises. (The identity of the freehold owners of the Scropton Lane industrial sites throughout their history has to date generally proved elusive).

The company was insolvent. It ceased trading on 31st July 1909 and was finally dissolved in 1912. But the factory itself continued to operate and it was presumably at this time that it was taken over by the British & Foreign Bottle Co as described by Mr Woolley.

• Wilfred Woolley is probably somewhere on the group photograph referred to above, and was one of a number of Hatton workers who transferred with the Anchor & Cross Bottle Works in 1910 to its new home in Kent. Queenborough on the Isle of Sheppey was the site of the newly-built Rushenden Industrial Estate, one of the earliest of its kind in the country (following the pioneering Trafford Park Estate in Manchester, and during what has been termed Britain's second Industrial Revolution). A Kent colleague of his, Mr Percy Farrow, provided more details of Wilfred's experience: *"He worked for two years at The Anchor & Cross factory as a presser followed by several years in the packing department, and when the factory moved to Queenborough in 1910 he came with it. Prior to the migration the company purchased land at Queenborough from the Queenborough Port & Development Co (known locally as "The Forty Thieves") and the first furnace house with a regenerative furnace fired with producer gas, equipped with ten Press & Blow machines and with a small warehouse attached, was almost ready to start production. A special train was obtained for the exercise and the whole personnel were moved lock, stock and barrel, complete with all goods and chattels, complete families with household pets, etc., and caused such consternation among the Island inhabitants that they thought they were being invaded.*

The Manager of the Anchor & Cross Works was a Mr Lamont and he moved to Queenborough in a like capacity. Later I understand he moved to Key Glass at New Cross and some of the employees moved with him. The Manager to follow him was Mr Wilfred Langwell. The gathering rings were never used at Queenborough, the furnaces being equipped with enclosed Potettes. From the foregoing it is obvious that the Anchor & Cross Works could only have made jars with a wide mouth suitable for pressing.

After transfer to Queenborough the Bottle Works was called "The Queenborough Glass Bottle Works Ltd" and was at some time taken over by "British Glass Industries" whose works and Head Office were at Stephenson Street, Canning Town, hence the name "Canning Town Glass Works Ltd".

● Anyone looking at the 1911 and 1921 Censuses of the Isle of Sheppey, without knowing of this episode, might understandably be puzzled by the large number of residents in this remote corner of Kent who had been born in faraway Hatton or Tutbury. Appendix E gives a list of those who had moved their "families, goods, chattels and household pets" on that Anchor & Cross special train in 1910. Typical 1911 examples were:

- Annie and John Corden aged 40, a General Labourer at a Glass Bottle Works. Boarding with them were our friend Wilfred Woolley aged 23, a Ware Sorter at the Works, their nephew Charles Drury aged 16, a Machine Operator at the Works and Joseph Kirkham aged 21, a Glass Gatherer, all born in Tutbury.

- George W Woolley, born in 1892 into the most extensive family of Tutbury glassworkers. He was living in 1911 in Rushenden with his widowed mother and siblings, working as a Gatherer at the Works. He was married on the Isle of Sheppey later that year to Daisy Walkman. Their son George T Woolley was born there in 1915. George junior found his way back to Tutbury by 1937 where he married Marjorie Wardle and as "Smack" Woolley became one of the best-known local Cutters of the Webb Corbett era.

On the morning of departure for Kent on 28th July 1910, the Burton Chronicle reporter was there as usual to provide his take:

"TUTBURY FAMILIES EXODUS
GLASS WORKERS LEAVE BY SPECIAL TRAIN

Monday morning witnessed an interesting exodus from Tutbury, about eighty of the inhabitants, comprising the whole of the employees of the Anchor & Cross Glass Works, leaving for Queenborough Kent, in consequence of the firm's removal of their works, joined the party and the scene on the station was an unusual one.

The Anchor & Cross works have now been closed down, the firm, which is to be known as the Queenborough Glass and Bottle Co., having removed the scene of their operations to the Kentish coast. This step is calculated to result in considerable saving, the drawback to the Tutbury Works being the cost of conveying the requisite sea sand thither. This, of course, can be had at Queenborough in great quantities, and new works have been erected there for the carrying on of the business.

The removal of the firm's employees en bloc was a natural sequence, and this morning a special train conveying them left Tutbury laden as well with all their household goods. There were about 12 vans of furniture, and there were many farewells as the train left for Burton en route for the south. At Burton, the Midland Railway Co took charge of the train, which was joined by a number of youths employed at the works. Many friends and relatives of the latter assembled to see them off, there being some affectionate leave-takings. The train was a heavy one, and the journey (via London) was expected to occupy the greater part of the day.

Although removing from the district the firm has not been unmindful of local industries, and it may be mentioned that the machinery for the new works at Queenborough has been supplied by Mr T H Baldock of Branstone Road, while Messrs Barnett & Sons have been responsible for the electric fittings.

The Anchor & Cross company have carried on business at works adjoining those formerly owned by Mr Richardson in Scropton Lane, Hatton. Their removal from the neighbourhood must of necessity be felt, but there is some little compensation in the fact that Messrs Corbett, who took over the old Tutbury Glassworks in the town, have acquired the premises previously owned by Mr Richardson in Scropton Lane, and are about to extend their business, while at the present they are more flush of orders [sic] than they have been for some time."

In total about eighty men, women and children left their homes in and around Hatton and Tutbury in 1910, a good many of them permanently. This economic mini-migration was probably unprecedented in the history of the villages and must have had quite an impact at the time. If nothing else, the departure of so many young men may have left a number of young ladies in tears, a forerunner of the real losses to be endured just a few years later during WW1.

And so ended the curious interlude of the Anchor & Cross Bottle Works in Hatton.

* * * * *

5.   1910-1920   Corbett & Co Ltd

What was probably the most turbulent time in the history of Hatton Glassworks followed. A charismatic salesman and perhaps the most colourful character in the story of glassmaking in Tutbury and Hatton, it is hard to know whether to portray George Harry Corbett as hero or villain.

He was born in 1856 in Kingswinford, near Stourbridge, his background fairly modest, his father a Shopkeeper. George worked his way up through the local glassmaking industry into both factory management and commercial roles. He went into partnership in the 1890's with Thomas Webb, whose family (along with the Richardsons and others) were part of the Stourbridge "glass aristocracy". The audacious Corbett and the genteel Webbs made an unlikely combination, but their business flourished on the back of their differing though complimentary talents. Thomas Webb retired because of mental ill-health in 1903 and was replaced at the head of the business by his younger brother, Herbert.

Following Thomas Webb & Corbett Ltd.'s acquisition of the Tutbury Glassworks in 1906, Corbett came from Stourbridge to manage the Ludgate Street factory on behalf of the firm. This he did over the next four years, and he must take considerable credit for shepherding the operation back from a near moribund state on the brink of bankruptcy to a position of stability and improved reputation, modelled on Webb Corbett's successful White House Glassworks in Wordsley.

But by 1910 George Harry Corbett was keen to be his own man. The exact circumstances of his departure from Thomas Webb & Corbett Ltd are not fully explained, but it seems that, whilst he was still their Tutbury Director, he had already put in motion his plans to set up on his own account and become the third "Pied Piper" (after Sivewright and Richardson) to make their way from Ludgate Street to Scropton Lane with an enthusiastic band of Tutbury Blowers and Cutters following behind.

* * * * *

A Bright New Dawn

By a Special Resolution at an Extraordinary General Meeting of shareholders held on 1st June 1910, Thomas Webb & Corbett Ltd resolved: *"That in exercise of the power conferred by article 22(1) of the Articles of Association of the company, Mr. George Harry Corbett be and he is hereby removed from the office of Managing Director of the company."* This was signed by Herbert Webb as Officer and Secretary. Corbett was replaced as a Director by George Edgar Heath, the company's London Sales Agent, and William Kny, the Works Manager at Stourbridge.

Figure 22 - View of Tutbury Glassworks from the Castle c.1910

84

On 20th June Webb wrote to Heath: *"Corbett ... is putting Richardson's old works in a state of repair...In last Saturday's local paper he was advertising his [Thomas Webb & Corbett Ltd} shares for sale."* Webb said that Corbett had made overtures to the Glass Blowers. But the Union was agreeing to effectively "black" the men and cancel their Union membership if they followed him. A deputation from the Union was going to go with Webb to Tutbury. Webb continued: *"Miss Corbett had given her notice, along with his brother, which I do not regret. I have learnt something which throws a light on Corbett's recent conduct..."*

It seems that the Union leaders back in Stourbridge were thick as thieves with the Webbs, but their proposed blacking of the Tutbury men was probably highly irregular. If they did pursue that, it did not deter a significant exodus to Hatton. Herbert Webb didn't go into print about what it was that threw "a light on Corbett's recent conduct." It may have been some business or financial matter, but equally likely it was his unorthodox personal life - his wife and two daughters had joined him in Tutbury, but he was simultaneously maintaining a long-term mistress and several other children by her back in Stourbridge. "Miss Corbett" was most likely his eldest daughter, Dora, aged 22, who had perhaps been working as a Clerk at Tutbury - by the time of the 1911 Census she was living at home, with no occupation given. His brother was Thomas Attwood Corbett who joined him at the Royal Castle Glassworks and appears three months later on the far right of an RCGW photograph as a slightly dandyish-looking Mould Maker.

• The photograph was taken outside the well-known Peveril of the Peak Hotel near Dovedale. It was dated by its donor Charles Crossley as 1910, in which case Corbett clearly lost no time in trying to coalesce his new group of skilled workers around him through a Works Outing - "bonding" on an "away-day" in modern jargon. The board at the front reads "Royal Castle Glass Works Tutbury".

Figure 23 - Corbett & Crew ready for action in the Dove Valley

Mr Crossley was able to assign partial names to all but three of the faces and, using censuses, parish records and Union registers, it has now been possible to confirm and expand these with personal details of the men. A full listing is given in Appendix F. Amongst those who figure specifically in this story of local glassmaking are:

George Harry Corbett, seated fourth left;
William Reynolds, to Corbett's left, his cashier and deputy manager;
George Woolley, the cameraman's friend, seated second left;
William Nicklin, master glassblower, middle row, third right;
Michael Molloy, FGMFS district president, bowler hatted, back row;
William Blood, High Court witness, middle row, fourth left;
Francis Crossley, master engraver, middle row, fifth left;
John Orchard, fellow engraver, seated third left;
Charles Marshall, RCGW caretaker, middle row second left, no hat;

Frank Pegg, the historian's friend, middle row, second right; Phillip and Harry McGuiness, back row, fourth left and middle row first left respectively, sons of the FGMFS stalwart, Phillip McGuiness senior.

[One of the authors was also thrilled to see, for the first time, an image of his maternal great grandfather Joe Siddalls senior, stern and bowler-hatted, fourth from the right in the middle row.]

This is the most iconic and informative of any employee photograph from the local glass industry. They form quite an impressive group of men, with the confidence and dignity that their craft skills gave them. Mr Corbett appears quietly satisfied, not to say smug, to have gathered them around him. Three further group pictures of the excursion have survived, one of them fortunately with all the men bare-headed, which is a great aid to identification. These other photos are more informal, taken out in the Peak District fields, one of them with the men "larking about" on donkeys - the managers, Corbett and Reynolds, do not appear in them, perhaps wanting to keep a little aloof. Several copies of the four photographs have come into the Museum's possession, the majority of them properly mounted. It was clearly a well-remembered day for many of the men, and the record of it survived in a number of local families.

Happily, a Burton Chronicle report of 22nd September 1910 confirms the dating and adds more colour to the day's events:

"TUTBURY. WORKMEN'S PICNIC. The workmen employed by Messrs. Corbett & Co., The Royal Castle Glass Works, had a most enjoyable picnic on Saturday last, the rendezvous chosen being Dovedale. The party drove in brakes provided by Mr C W Dunn, High Street, Tutbury, and started shortly after 9 a.m., proceeding via Foston, Cubley and Ashbourne to the Peveril Hotel, where dinner was

provided. Ample justice having been done to the repast, Thorpe Cloud, Reynard's Cave and, by the more adventurous spirits, the Dove Holes were visited. The Dale is glorious at all times, but in the early autumn, with its myriad tints, changing from pale yellow to orange, splashed with crimson, it is superb, and the present time is the most propitious for seeing it in all its radiant beauty. Tea was partaken of at the Peveril, and at the conclusion Mr G H Corbett made one of his effective little speeches. The return journey was begun shortly after six o'clock. On reaching Cubley Inn a short halt was made for refreshments. Mr W Nicklin gave an excellent rendering of the old favourite song "The old wooden rocker" and Mr P McGuinness was equally effective in "The old Turnkey". Tutbury was reached about 10 p.m., thus bringing to a close the first of what is trusted will be a long series of these annual outings."

- Corbett's new venture ran for the first few months as an unincorporated business trading as Corbett & Co, but on 13th May 1911 he formed a limited company "Corbett and Company Limited". Its Objects in the Memorandum of Association were: *"(a) To acquire and take over as a going concern the business of a Glass Worker and Manufacturer of Glass now carried on by George Harry Corbett at Hatton in the County of Derby, under the style or firm of "CORBETT & COMPANY", together with the whole of the assets and liabilities of the proprietor...(b) To carry on, either in connection with business aforesaid, or as distinct and separate businesses, the business or businesses of Glass Workers and Manufacturers of Glass of all kinds..."* (This just happens to mirror very closely the Memorandum of Thomas Webb & Corbett Ltd).

The company had an authorized share capital of £7,000. Three thousand shares were allotted to GHC in consideration for the transfer of his business, and a further one thousand five hundred shares were issued for cash between three acquaintances of his, Joseph Darby, a

Glass & China Merchant of Nottingham, Alfred Smith, a retired Farmer from Anslow, and Alfred Hingley, a Commercial Traveller of Brierley Hill. These three were appointed Directors, along with Corbett as Managing Director. He had a two thirds majority shareholding at that stage. From later evidence, Darby was the most active of Corbett's partners in the venture. Both he and Smith had helped to finance Corbett whilst he was operating in the first few months as a sole trader.

- After its incorporation the company immediately executed an Indenture for the purchase of Corbett's unincorporated business. The key terms were as follows:

"WHEREAS the Vendor [Corbett] is now carrying on business as a flint glass manufacturer on the premises described in the Schedule hereto under the style of "Corbett & Company", and WHEREAS the Vendor has entered into an Agreement with the Executors of James Eadie deceased for the purchase of the said premises...including the plant and fixtures...at the price of £1,500...IT IS HEREBY AGREED as follows: -

1. The Vendor shall sell and the Company shall purchase: -

(a) The interest of the Vendor in the said Agreement for Purchase...

(b) The goodwill of the business with the exclusive right to use the name "Corbett"...and all patents, trade-marks, designs and licences...

(c) All the plant, machinery, office furniture, stock-in-trade, implements and utensils...

(d) All the book and other debts due to the Vendor...

(e) The full benefit of all pending contacts and engagements...

(f) All cash in hand and at bank and all bills and notes of the Vendor...

(g) All other property to which the Vendor is entitled in connection with the said business.

2. Part of the consideration for the said sale shall be the sum of £3,000 which shall be satisfied by the allotment to the Vendor of 3,000 fully paid-up shares of the Company of £1...

3. As to the residue of the consideration...the Company shall undertake to pay...all debts...of the Vendor in relation to the said business.

4. The sale...is intended to take effect as a sale...as a going concern as from January 1st.1911. ...

10. The Vendor shall be the first managing director of the Company...[salary to be agreed]...[with a non-compete clause]...provided always that nothing herein contained shall prevent the Vendor from carrying on or being engaged or concerned or interested to a reasonable extent in the manufacture of glass of a different quality from that now manufactured by the Vendor...and the Vendor shall be at liberty to devote to any such other business or manufacture such a reasonable amount of his time as shall be consistent with his duties as Managing Director of the Company...

11. The Vendor shall...retain at least 2,000 of the shares...for a period of ten years... [Initially drafted as 3,000, manuscript amendment initialled by GHC and JTD].

12. The Company shall pay all costs...."

The Schedule referred to*: "All that piece or parcel of land containing by admeasurement 4,959 square yards...at Hatton...together with the buildings erected thereon and formerly known as the New Glass Works but now known as The Royal Castle Glass Works...formerly in the occupation of John Thomas Haden Richardson..."*

• The Works would clearly have needed a good deal of refurbishment as it is likely that they had not been used for production purposes for ten years. Renovation and refiring of the furnaces, together with re-establishment of the cutting and engraving processes would have been quite a significant undertaking for Corbett. The ageing JTH

Richardson must have looked on with very mixed feelings from his nearby house.

- The Indenture is the first and to date the only known reference to the role of James Eadie in the Hatton Glassworks. Of Scottish origin, he established a substantial brewery in Burton-on-Trent in the second half of the 19th century. He lived with his family at Barrow Hall, Barrow-on-Trent, Derbyshire, some ten miles from Hatton. He died in June 1904, leaving an estate of £337,000. His sons carried on the business, which was eventually acquired by Bass, Ratcliffe and Gretton in 1933. Eadie had an existing property interest in Hatton, still recalled today on the prominent sign on the corner of the Railway Inn in Station Road, which records the purchase of the public house by James Eadie's brewery in 1887.

It is not yet known with certainty when Eadie acquired the freehold of the Royal Castle Glass Works site – whether after it had closed around 1900, or if he had had an earlier financial interest in the business when it was being operated by the Richardson family. Interestingly, his son William Stewart Eadie was a leading local cricketer whose county career with Derbyshire coincided with that of Tom Richardson. Doubtless, the two would have been well acquainted and this may have provided the initiative for business connections between the two families.

The most obvious answer is that James Eadie was the purchaser of the RCGW freehold at the auction sale held in 1896 (see Chapter 3). It is also possible that Eadie's Brewery was a customer of the RCGW in the late 19th century. Many of the leading Burton breweries were also using Jackson's Tutbury factory as a supplier of glassware for their tied public houses, and in 1880 the Ludgate Street factory itself provided an example of brewing interests actually investing in a local glassworks.

91

• The "non-compete" covenant in Clause 10 of the Indenture is significant. The qualification it contains effectively granted Corbett a very unusual degree of freedom to get up to whatever else he liked in the industry. He may have had it inserted to avoid what had got him into trouble with the Webbs, but it was surely a potential recipe for further friction that his fellow shareholders would have been well advised to exclude from the Agreement.

• And so, Corbett & Co Ltd was launched into the bright new dawn heralded in the faces on that Dovedale excursion - though that might have been the effects of the liquor as well. For its new letterhead the company adopted the same engraving of the Royal Castle Glass Works that Richardson had commissioned in 1879.

The 1911 Census, in conjunction with the 1910 photographs, provides sufficient data to build up a good picture of the company's workforce:

- Twelve of the thirty-two men pictured are Blowers - Michael Molloy, Phillip McGuinness, William Nicklin Snr, Harry McGuinness, James Woolley, James Cooke, James Corfield, William Pavey, Thomas Woolley, George Woolley, George Compson and William Nicklin Jnr;

- Nine are Decorators - Cutters Charles Marshall, John Lock, Joseph Scotton, William Barker, Joseph Siddalls, Arthur Barker and Richard Irons; plus Etcher/Engraver Francis Crossley and a second Engraver, John Orchard;

- Six are support staff - Mould Maker, Thomas Attwood Corbett; Engineer's Fitter, Frank Pegg; Joiner, William Blood; Teazer, Samuel Sharp; Packer, George Cresswell; Clerk Samuel Siddalls;

- Of the remaining five, there is George Harry Corbett himself and his Manager William Reynolds, plus three unknowns.

It is likely that Corbett would also have employed a number of boys. It was a men-only outing of course, and no doubt he had female staff as well, who were not invited. Three people on the 1911 Census specifically gave their employer as Corbett & Co, but do not appear on the photograph - Mary Ann Rudge, a 24-year-old Glass Warehouse Woman, Bert Preston, a 17-year-old Cutter, and George Sheppard, a 19-year-old apprentice Blower. In addition, on the Census there were no fewer than eleven young apprentice Glass Cutters, living in Hatton, who don't give their employer's name, but most of them were very probably working for Corbett.

In total, therefore, he was employing in the order of fifty workers by 1911, which was very much the norm for the Hatton and Tutbury factories in the nineteenth and early twentieth centuries. The large majority were locally born, and Corbett clearly did not have to go far afield to recruit the skills he needed. All in all, it was a comprehensive and capable workforce to have built up in just a few months.

• Meanwhile the Webb Corbett shop floor in Ludgate Street was left leaderless and half empty. John Webb despatched one of his lieutenants from the Stourbridge headquarters, Walter Guest, to pick up the management reins, no doubt with some skilled Stourbridge hands to keep the production running temporarily – on the 1911 Census for example there were at least twenty glassworkers in Tutbury who had Black Country birthplaces, significantly quite a number of them living as Boarders and Lodgers.

It must have been a tough assignment for Guest, but he was a tough man. He never went back and continued to manage the Tutbury Glassworks through forty successful years until his retirement in the early 1950's, when he was succeeded by his son, Paul Guest.

• Few details have yet come to light of Corbett & Co's production and sales in the pre-WW1 years. Frank Pegg recalled that they "made tableware which was engraved. It was lightly blown lead glass and the engraving was of a very high standard." Francis Crossley was the most celebrated local etcher and engraver, and his skills were passed on to his son Charles.

Of the following collection, clockwise from the left, numbers one, three and seven are the work of Francis; numbers two, four and five of Charles; and number six by William Orchard.

Figure 24 - RCGW glass from the Corbett & Co era

The lightness and delicacy of the glass stands out. A second collection gives examples of work by a wider range of RCGW craftsmen:

94

Figure 25 - More of RCGW's finest

The first two glasses on the left were engraved by John Orchard; the third by E Holt, and the one on the right by William Orchard, son of John. All were blown by William Nicklin and acid polished by Francis Crossley, and date from around 1910. The fine bowl second from the right is much earlier, about 1880, engraved by the Bohemian, Frederick August Bohm.

* * * * *

Stormy Weather

The company soon needed more money. In November 1911 four hundred and forty new shares in Corbett & Co Ltd were issued for cash to Joseph Darby and a mortgage loan was taken out from Lloyds

Bank. The Lloyds loan was redeemed in July 1912 from the proceeds of a £500 loan from George Lewis Gent, a Glass & China Dealer of Holborn Circus, London (who also held shares in Thomas Webb & Corbett Ltd). Shortly before, in April 1912, a further two thousand new shares had been issued to Gent for cash. Corbett no longer held a majority shareholding after this time.

The new funds raised may have been for development and expansion of the business. But, more likely, it had been a struggle from the start and there was insufficient working capital behind the operation to succeed. The company increased its turnover every half year, but never produced a profit or a dividend. Corbett's focus was no doubt on sales, and the less glamorous grind of controlling finances and keeping down production costs was perhaps neglected. The Tutbury Blowers and Cutters may have been enticed to Hatton not just by his personal charisma, but also by higher wages than the business could afford. Commercial antagonism from the powerful Webbs should not be discounted either, channelled through the energetic and uncompromising Walter Guest now in charge in Ludgate Street.

By early 1913 George Harry Corbett was in serious trouble.

• Enter Stanley Noel Jenkinson. Although earlier sketches of the history of the Hatton Glassworks have dated Jenkinson's involvement from 1916, it is now clear from Companies House filings and press reports that he took control of Corbett & Co Ltd in 1913 and that Corbett was ousted in that year.

Jenkinson (1886-1982) was the third generation of his family at the head of the successful Edinburgh & Leith Flint Glass Company Ltd. He was approached to help the Hatton company in its financial difficulties, and according to later Court reports the Scot acquired all the shares in Corbett & Co Ltd for cash on 13th May 1913 following completion of a "distributing agreement". On 10th June a new Company Secretary, Charles Tod, informed Companies House that Corbett, Darby and Smith had resigned as Directors, replaced by Stanley Jenkinson and Charles Green, a China Merchant and Agent of Hatton Garden, London. Tod was also from Edinburgh and took over as Works Manager at Hatton on behalf of Jenkinson. He was almost certainly the Charles Tod, born 1874, working as a Glass Warehouseman in Edinburgh on the 1891 and 1901 Censuses of Scotland. His mother was born Margaret Jenkinson, in Leith, possibly giving him family ties to the Stanley Jenkinson family.

The plan was that Corbett would continue employment with the company in a sales capacity. But it didn't work out and he was soon obliged to leave the firm. His response was to take the company and his former shareholder colleagues to Court for wrongful dismissal, conspiracy to defraud him of the value of his shares, and forcing him out of the company to his ruin. The Midlands and Edinburgh press reported on the case, eventually heard in early 1915 in the King's Bench Division of the High Court in London.

• Extensive transcripts of the newspaper reports on the legal proceedings can be found in Tutbury Museum's archives (ref GL397), and give a quite comprehensive account of events. The Press coverage of the case was surprisingly prominent, given that the War was in full flow, and the "Tutbury Glassworks Litigation" competed successfully for front page space with "The Forcing of the Dardanelles", the notorious "Brides in the Bath" murder trial of George Smith, and the dreadful casualty lists from the Western Front. On the day the jury gave its judgment, for example, nine hundred and seventy-one military casualties were reported, half of them killed, which puts Mr Corbett's travails into context. (Amongst the wounded was a Lieutenant W W Tod of the Royal Scots Fusiliers, which might possibly have given Charles Tod a double reason to despair).

The basis of the fraud charges laid by Corbett was that he had been coerced by his fellow directors and shareholders, Darby, Gent and Smith, into selling his shares at an under-value - Jenkinson paid just ten shillings per £1 share, and in addition Corbett had been obliged to give £585 out of the consideration he received to the other shareholders. This had been done, he claimed, under threats of putting the company into liquidation and of proceedings against him for issuing a false balance sheet to induce Gent to originally invest in the business.

He was rather handicapped in his claims, however, as he had agreed to the sale arrangements in writing. His counter to this was that he was suffering from ill health and was in a state of collapse at the time. In Court, the other directors said they had personal sympathy with Corbett, but had no confidence in him to ever make a success of the business. In 1913, they maintained, the company had been in a critical financial position, and the offer from Jenkinson was the only way to avoid liquidation. Jenkinson himself regretted ever having entered into the agreement as he felt "he had been had".

The case lasted eight days in February and March 1915, interrupted by Mr Justice Lawrence's absence to preside at Manchester Assizes. The judge was frustrated by the drawn-out proceedings, remarking on one occasion that "the case would ruin everybody".

When the jury's decision finally came on Friday 5th March it was to award Corbett judgement against the company of £250 for wrongful dismissal and £735 against Messrs Darby, Gent and Smith for conspiracy. His action against Jenkinson was rejected. The defendants immediately indicated their intention to appeal and pleaded with the judge for a stay of execution from paying the damages and costs. The judge refused.

On the basis of the case as reported, the conspiracy judgment seems a perverse decision, with little evidence to support the view that Darby and Gent had actively worked together to unlawfully force Corbett out of his shareholding and employment. They were just shareholders legitimately trying to limit their losses in a failing company by finding the best price they could for their shares. Smith, a retired farmer, was very much a passive player, having put money into the company on the basis of Corbett's blandishments that "it would be a good investment for the wife". But somehow the old Corbett charisma must have resurfaced to win over the jury to his side.

• Whether the damages matched Corbett's hopes for compensation one cannot tell, but he must surely have enjoyed this initial vindication. However, his enjoyment could not have lasted much more than twenty-four hours. The defendants, no doubt shocked by the verdict, were in the Court of Appeal on the Saturday morning, pleading at this higher level for a stay of action until their appeal was heard. They were willing to pay their money into the Court, but feared that if it was paid out to Mr Corbett they might never recover it in the event of their appeal succeeding. Corbett's counsel retorted that his client was now a poor man, because the defendants had ruined his business, but that he was not penniless.

The Appeal Court judges were persuaded by the defence and on the following Monday ruled that the money should be paid into Court. Corbett was permitted to receive £3 per week until the outcome of the appeal.

It took nearly a year for the appeal to be heard. The Derby Daily Telegraph reported on 13th January 1916:

"THE TUTBURY GLASS-WORKS LITIGATION
APPEAL OF THE DEFENDANTS OPENED

In the Court of Appeal on Wednesday, before Lords Justices Swinfen Eady, Pickford and Bankes, the appeal by the defendants, other than the defendant Jenkinson, from a verdict and judgement entered against them at the trial in the case of Corbett v Corbett & Co Ltd and others, was opened.

Mr McCall for the appellants said the plaintiff was George Harry Corbett, glass manufacturer, Tutbury, and the defendants were Corbett & Co Ltd whose registered office was at Hatton, Derbyshire, Joseph Thomas Darby, George Lewis Gent, Stanley Noel Jenkinson, and Alfred Smith. The plaintiff claimed damages as against the company for alleged breach of contract, as against the other defendants for maliciously procuring such alleged breach, and as against all the defendants for alleged conspiracy. As regarded Mr Jenkinson judgement was entered for him, and therefore he was not a party to the appeal, although he was interested in a so-called cross-appeal.

The result of the action, which lasted several days before Mr Justice A T Lawrence and a special jury was a verdict and judgement for £735 against Messrs Darby, Gent and Smith for conspiracy and £250 for wrongful dismissal. The ground of the appeal was misdirection and a [illegible] on the facts as found by the jury there was no case of "coercion", "threat" or "duress" upon which the plaintiff had founded his claim for damages.

Counsel narrated the circumstances in which the plaintiff and friends in 1911 transferred the glassworks at Tutbury to a company called Corbett & Co Ltd. In 1913, he said, the company disposed of the whole of the shares to Mr Jenkinson, a glass manufacturer in Edinburgh, and Mr Corbett agreed to become a director [sic]. There was [illegible] controversy with regard to Corbett's shares and later

100

the plaintiff brought the action alleging that he had only agreed to transfer under threat that if he stood out the company would be wound up. Counsel contended that the plaintiff had not been coerced, and that there was no case of action.

The hearing was adjourned."

The Derby Telegraph reported the outcome of the appeal on 21st February 1916:

"THE TUTBURY GLASS CO DISPUTE
The Appeal Court on Friday allowed the appeal by John Thomas Darby, Nottingham, George Lewis Gent, London, and Alfred Smith, Anslow, near Burton, three former directors of Corbett and Co Ltd., glass manufacturers, Tutbury, against the verdict and judgement for £735 upon a claim by Mr G H Corbett, former managing director, for damages for alleged conspiracy, threats, and duress, whereby he said he was induced to part with his shares in the company at a gross under-value when the concern was taken over by Stanley Noel Jenkinson, Queen Street, Edinburgh. Judgement was entered for the defendants, with costs."

There is no reference to any appeal by the Company against the award of £250 for wrongful dismissal, and this was probably not pursued. But £250 would surely have been little solace to Corbett in the face of the dreaded word "costs" of this lengthy litigation, which he was ordered to bear and which may well have ruined him.

• The actual date of his dismissal from "his" company is not evident, but it appears to have been back in 1913, for on 20th December of that year the Telegraph reported:

"It was announced yesterday by the Commercial Development Committee of Burton-on-Trent Corporation that another new industry had been secured for the town. Mr G H Corbett, of Tutbury and Stourbridge, it was stated, had leased premises in Byrkley Street, in which to carry on the business of glass decorating and engraving, and that in future a large number of hands would be employed. Arrangements had been made with a large American firm for supplying blanks of plain glass vessels made by a new process.

It was not at all unlikely that more extensive premises would have to be taken, as a big trade development was expected by reason of Mr Corbett's arrangement with the American firm, including the right to supply the whole of Europe with this special class of glassware. Mr Corbett has supplied the King and Prince of Wales with a sample of the decorated glass which is to be made at Burton, and also many famous Atlantic liners. Later rock crystal engraving, the highest and most skilled branch of the decorator's art, is to be introduced."

No evidence has been found that anything ever came of all this. Mr Corbett knew how to supply a journalist with good copy and the report could stand as an epitaph to his unflagging energy, optimism and salesmanship, alongside an addiction to grandiose plans.

• Then approaching sixty, his business career probably never recovered from the events in Hatton. His later life was punctuated by the occasional registration of glass patents, and campaigns against others who he felt had wronged him.

Perhaps the great irony of his life is that his name was never dropped by the company from which he parted acrimoniously in 1910 and which went on to trade so notably as Webb Corbett for much of the rest of the century. If he had only negotiated a modest lifelong "royalty" agreement at the time for the use of his name, it would surely have brought him much more reward and much less grief than Corbett & Co ever did.

George Harry Corbett died in Halesowen, Worcestershire in 1948 aged 94.

Figure 26 - GHC in old age

Some years ago, this fine photograph of him in old age stood in the Webb Corbett Visitor Centre (now the Glasshouse Heritage Centre) in Stourbridge - immaculately dressed, walking cane in hand, and with the hint of a wistful smile on his face. Though he may have lost some battles along the way, he does not appear to have lost his style.

The Hatton Glassmaking story is not a tale of villainy, but rather one of heroic failures. In just three years of operations in Scropton Lane, Corbett packed in more energy and drama than many do in a lifetime. He deserves to be remembered positively.

* * * * *

Corporate Manoeuvring

But we must return to Stanley Noel Jenkinson, left reluctantly with Corbett & Co Ltd on his hands in 1913. It is a further irony that, after this equally acrimonious parting, Jenkinson also continued to trade under the Corbett name for a further six years.

• Looking first at the formal affairs of the company, there followed a series of changes in shareholdings and directors over the remainder of Corbett & Co Ltd.'s brief existence:

- In November 1914 a further 1,000 5% preference shares were created and issued to John Ferguson and Dugald Smith, Merchants of London.
- In December 1914 the Registered Office was moved from Scropton Lane, Hatton to 49 Hatton Gardens, London. (Yet more irony, as the two locations could hardly be more different).
- In the same month an additional Director was appointed, John Scoular, an Engineer of the Omega Lamp Works, Hammersmith, London. John Weller, Cashier to Charles Green's London business, was acting as Company Secretary by then.
- In July 1915, Charles Tod, Works Manager at Hatton, joined the Board of Directors.
- In March 1916, Weller was made up to Director as well, replacing Charles Green and John Scoular.
- Following this, all shares in the company were in the names of Jenkinson and his wife Edith, with the exception of 500 held by Tod and 200 by a Henry H Pitt, a Merchant from County Durham.
- In the next three years a further 5,000 shares were issued for cash, mainly to the Jenkinson family and associates, but including very small parcels of shares to some of his key workers - an early example of employee shareholder participation. Was Jenkinson a generous,

progressive employer or was it just a cynical way to keep the Hatton troops happy?

- Amongst the recipients were Charles Tod; William Jeremiah Scriven of 29 Bridge Street, Tutbury, a Tube Drawer; John Bentley of 34 Cornmill Lane, Tutbury, also a Tube Drawer; and John William Reynolds of 10 Church Street, Tutbury, the Assistant Manager at the RCGW, Corbett's former right-hand man, who had clearly survived the downfall of his boss.

- In August 1916 a further Director was appointed, Robert Woolmer Johnston, a Glass Manufacturer of Sydenham, Kent.

The overall picture to be deduced is of Jenkinson in control from his headquarters in Edinburgh, aided on site by local managers he had appointed. Additional funds were invested in the business and he sought a series of alliances with other players in the glass trade.

• As regards the production operations of Corbett & Co Ltd in the years following 1913, two things stand out. The first defining event was the switch of production to electric light bulb and tube blowing during the course of World War One. This story overlaps with the involvement of British Thomson-Houston and is told in the next chapter.

• Secondly, in 1916/7, there was a major rebuilding of part of the works to create a new Glasshouse, incorporating modern Hermansen furnaces - one a six-pot, the other an eight-pot. The following photograph shows the new building approaching its completion.

Tutbury Museum holds Architect's plans and drawings for the structure. This appears to have replaced the main two storey building on the left of the 1879 engraving - the piles of brick rubble in the foreground may be the residue of its demolition.

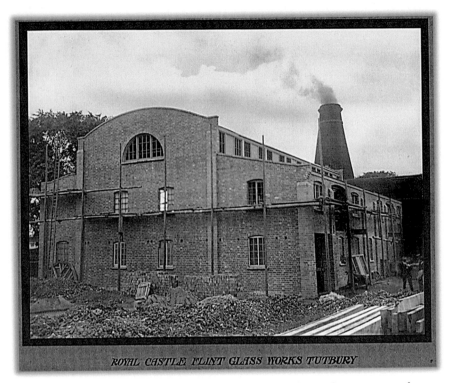

ROYAL CASTLE FLINT GLASS WORKS TUTBURY

Figure 27 - Construction of new RCGW Glasshouse nearing completion in 1917

The photograph is taken in the same direction as the engraving, from the Scropton Lane frontage looking south towards the railway line. One of the old furnace chimneys can be seen. The roofed structure running at right angles to the rear is marked on the plans as an "existing warehouse", and may possibly be part of Sivewright's original Works. The new Glasshouse, built within wartime constraints, did not win any aesthetic prizes. But it provided an improved setting for an increase in the production of light bulbs, and in later years formed a core part of the Trent Valley operation. At a later stage, the date at present unknown, the lateral "aisles" and central walls were replaced by wooden structures of similar dimensions. These were destroyed in a 1971 fire, leaving just the arched end walls standing.

- The factory workforce appears to have escaped relatively unscathed by World War One. Whilst all the other major local employers, including Webb Corbett, saw a number of their men killed, only one casualty from Corbett & Co has so far been identified - Bert Preston, a Glass Cutter from Hatton when he enlisted in the Territorial Army in 1912, and who fell along with so many of his 6th Battalion North Staffordshire Regiment colleagues in the killing ground in front of Gommecourt Wood on 1st July 1916, the first day of the Battle of the Somme.

Mention can be also made of George Henry Siddalls (son of Joe Siddalls), a Private in the Middlesex Regiment, missing in action in northern France on 28th August 1918 - in 1911 he was one of the apprentice Cutters from Hatton presumed to be working for Corbett, though by the time of his enlistment he had joined Nestlé's Dairy. Additionally, Edward Woolley who moved to Kent with his mother and brothers from Tutbury in 1910 and later worked at the Queenborough Glassworks was also a casualty, killed on the Somme in July 1916.

- At the beginning of 1920, the Hatton enterprise was amalgamated into a major new national grouping of glassmakers, called Webb's Crystal Glass Company Ltd, a subsidiary of British Glass Industries Ltd. Several of the companies brought together had some distant thread connecting them to Tutbury or Hatton:

- Thomas Webb & Son Ltd, best known of the Webb family Stourbridge businesses, of which Thomas Webb & Corbett Ltd had been an early offshoot;

- British Glass Industries Ltd, Medway Glass Works Ltd and United Glass Bottle Manufacturers of Canning Town, each with connections to the Anchor & Cross Bottle Works;
- Edinburgh & Leith Flint Glass Company Ltd, Jenkinson's home base; and
- Corbett & Co Ltd itself.

Corbett & Co was hardly big enough to have been a key element in the project, and it is more likely that Jenkinson just threw the Hatton factory "into the mix" along with his Edinburgh & Leith company. The transaction was in the form of the sale of the assets of Corbett & Co Ltd in exchange for a mixture of cash and shares in Webb's Crystal Glass Company Ltd. This was authorised by a Special Resolution of Corbett & Co Ltd dated 19th February 1920 and signed by Jenkinson.

The shares allotted comprised 8,226 £1 Preference Shares and 8,226 1/- Ordinary Shares. The market value attributable to the Ordinary Shares and the amount of the cash consideration is not known, but it appears that Jenkinson got at least some return on his investment and that the company was a going concern at the time of sale.

• Both Stanley Jenkinson and Robert Johnston were involved in the promotion of Webb's Crystal Glass Company Ltd. In the background, as a Director of the parent company, British Glass Industries Ltd, also loomed large the figure of Clarence Charles Hatry.

Hatry was in some ways the Robert Maxwell of his day. Formerly an Insurance Clerk, he had become a wealthy company promoter during World War One. Hatry pursued an extravagant nouveau riche lifestyle in Mayfair during the 1920's. His speciality was the creation of industry groupings in the manner of Webb's Crystal Glass. He finally overreached himself in 1929 when trying to put together a giant iron and steel merger. His finances under pressure, he resorted to issuing fraudulent securities to keep his companies afloat. The Bank of England got wind of this, he owned up to the authorities, and his commercial empire collapsed with a deficit of $145 million. He was jailed for fourteen years for fraud. The insolvency is regarded by some as one of the factors in the loss of investor confidence that led to the Wall Street Crash.

• After the asset sale to Webbs Crystal Glass back in 1920, Corbett & Co Ltd, now a shell company, went into Voluntary Liquidation and its shares in Webbs were distributed to the shareholders. The Liquidator, Mr John Henry Trease of Nottingham, held the final Winding Up Meeting of Corbett & Co Ltd on 26th August 1920.

Corbett & Co Ltd thus ended its short and turbulent corporate life. But the Royal Castle Glass Works was still there physically of course in 1920, blowing glass in Hatton. It lasted just a little longer before its own demise as part of an operational re-organisation within the British Thomson-Houston group.

* * * * *

6.   1914-1924   British Thomson-Houston Co Ltd

British Thomson-Houston Co Ltd ("BTH") never owned the Hatton Glassworks, but for a period of ten years it played a key part in the factory's affairs, involving the switch of production from traditional decorated tableware to electric light bulbs.

• BTH was a major manufacturer of electric power related equipment, connected to General Electric in the USA. They first commenced the manufacture of electrical lamps in the UK on a limited scale in 1902. Their supplies of basic glass bulbs and tubing came from Germany and Austria. Instability of the tungsten filaments was a major difficulty for BTH and in 1911 they acquired patents from America for making drawn wire filaments, plus the trade name "Mazda". Sales then expanded substantially.

With the outbreak of World War One the German and Austrian supply chain was closed off. Some alternative supplies were available from the USA, but the British authorities were faced with the need to rapidly establish a viable home industry. This was mainly directed through BTH, headquartered in Rugby. Bulbs were made of lead glass and BTH looked for suppliers among the numerous small glass factories then producing domestic lead crystal tableware.

• The Hatton factory was one of those approached and Jenkinson agreed to switch part of his production to bulb and tube blowing. For many glass manufacturers it proved a testing transition. Any inconsistency in the glass caused problems for the lamp makers, as glass-to-glass and glass-to-metal sealing techniques required very careful control of the glass composition. Hatton had initial problems of a different sort however, as the existing glass blowers seemed unwilling to compromise on the use of their craft skills and associated pay rates.

Charles Tod, Jenkinson's Hatton Manager, wrote first on 10th September 1914 to Philip McGuiness, the Hatton "Factory Secretary" of the glassblowers' Union (by then called The National Flint Glass Makers Society of Great Britain and Ireland) to explain the plans for light bulb production:

"Dear McGuiness

I have been asked by my directors to intimate officially that [BTH] have taken an interest in our business, and a representative of their firm is joining the Board of Corbett and Co., Ltd.   On their behalf we are undertaking the manufacture of electric bulbs.   They require exceedingly large quantities, and to begin with, we are lighting our 12-pot furnace.   This, of course, will only supply a part of their requirements.

If your Society has any labour suitable we would be pleased to have their names and ages of the men, and where they have experience of this work.   They will work day and night shifts, with foot operated moulds and iron cleaning machines will be used as soon as we can obtain supplies.   With the help of the government, it is proposed to bring over a few men from the Continent who have been thrown idle owing to the war. These men will form a nucleus, and around them we will build up, as fast as we can, a factory worked with local labour, as naturally, it would take some time to teach young men. If you have suitable labour, kindly let us have a list of the names inside a week, as the matter is most urgent.   The rate of wages paid will be the normal one, namely, for the 25 and 32 Watts, 10d per hundred, and 5d per hundred for the pick-outs will be paid, and the larger sizes in proportion.   We are also pleased to inform you that this will be a permanent trade, and will continue after the war is finished. For your guidance, we might mention that [BTH] are an exceedingly large and very business-like firm, and are making every effort to start without delay.

We also wish to make it perfectly clear that it is not proposed to interfere in any way with our present trade. Our hand-made Chairs will continue to work as before."

In a repeat of the Richardson days in the 1800's, the Union's General Secretary, another Husselbee, quickly came from Birmingham to Hatton to discuss this with his members. The Union's initial response was that, as long as prevailing rates of pay were maintained and they could not supply the skilled labour themselves, then they had no objection to the engagement of foreigners, providing they joined the Union.

Within a few weeks, however, the two sides, or perhaps more particularly Jenkinson and Husselbee, had managed to acrimoniously and publicly fall out. The men went back on their agreement and went on strike in the face of the arrival of bulb blowers from abroad. Which side was actually to blame is not clear. For the management, perhaps it was wartime tension (the War was clearly not "going to be over by Christmas"), and the unsettling Corbett litigation was simmering in the background. Jenkinson went so far as to write to the Editor of the Burton Chronicle, asking him to publish the Company/Union correspondence, with its accusations of lack of patriotism thrown in. On 24th December 1914 the Editor obliged.

Frank Pegg recalled that *"eight blowers and two tube-drawers, together with a Belgian Interpreter, were brought over from Choissy le Roi, near Paris"*, and that it was from their efforts that bulbs were first successfully blown at Hatton. The striking native blowers were sacked, the men being dispersed by the Union to other glassworks across the country. Frank Pegg dated the start of bulb-blowing in Hatton as being in 1917 and this has been repeated subsequently. However, the documentary evidence indicates that arrangements were in place as early as 1914, though actual production may not have started until 1915. It is noteworthy also that the new BTH-appointed director who Tod referred to appears to be John Scoular, who joined in December 1914, describing himself as an Engineer of the Omega Lamp Works, Hammersmith, and presumably a man with knowledge of the light bulb industry.

• The bulb production process was described in "The Hatton Glassmakers" as follows:

"The Tutbury works consisted of a six pot Hermansen furnace, using closed pots of 10 cwts. capacity and direct coal firing. A lead glass was employed for both tubing and bulbs, not vastly different from the composition of normal crystal glass. Manufacture of spherical bulbs mainly of 60 mm. diameter was undertaken by the use of semi-automatic "Empire" machines. Each machine had four blowing positions which a hand gatherer kept supplied by placing the blowing iron with its gob of glass in a horizontal rotating chuck and adjustable marver plate. After marvering, the glass eventually swung to the vertical position with the elongating glass blank facing downwards into a two-part mould, the closing of which was done by a boy who, after completion of the blowing cycle, took out the blowing iron with bulb attached and, with a file and a tap on the iron, detached the bulb onto a bench. Production was of the order of 2,000 bulbs per machine per eight hours.

Tubing was made by hand, a large gather of glass on a large blowing iron was marvered and blown to the required shape by a hand blower and, by reheating the blank, the hand blower was able to attach a flat punty to the end of the glass blank and then proceeded to withdraw backwards with the punty in front of him and in full view of the stationary "mate" holding the original blowing iron, who at a signal from the "drawer" supplied the necessary air by mouth to produce a remarkable yield of tubing within 1mm of requirements."

• The correct dating of the commencement of bulb production is of interest in relation to the major factory reconstruction in 1916/17. Traditional tableware sales would surely not have been flourishing sufficiently during wartime to justify such an investment. It is likely that the expansion was on the back of significant bulb production. The Works were electrified later in 1917, in support of the Empire bulb-blowing machines.

The photograph opposite has been previously dated to the 1920s or 30s. If so, the replacement of brick by wood in the side "aisles" and upper storey side walls (referred to above) would presumably have taken place in the brief window between 1917 and the end of production in 1924.

ROYAL CASTLE FLINT GLASS WORKS TUTBURY

Figure 28 - The factory in its bulb-blowing days?

• It is not known if production was devoted 100% to bulb and tube production by the time of the Webbs Crystal Glass Ltd amalgamation, or whether an element of traditional tableware was still being made. Aubrey Bailey states that *"During this period in the Work's history, dolls eyes and tubular glass were manufactured, the latter for making into capsules which were sewn into soldiers' tunics and also for indicator*

114

glasses for use on steam engines." Syringes and glass cigarette holders are also recalled.

• It appears that Webbs Crystal Glass initially had local ambitions to expand their operations, as on 10th March 1920 they made a surprising purchase at auction of Park Hill House at the top of Castle Street, Tutbury together with a substantial adjoining plot of land, paying £1,300. The land is now the site of the five private houses that run along Park Lane between Park Hill House and the Council Houses built in the 1930s.

Park Lane at the time was completely undeveloped and the most likely explanation is that Webbs had plans to build some new facility there. Certainly, Clarence Hatry was pursuing acquisitions and developments at breakneck speed across his glass-making conglomerate at the time. But any such plans came to nothing as within a year they had resold the land to Tutbury Rural District Council, who sub-divided the plot for later development of the private housing. Park Hill House itself was sold in 1925.

This appears to signal the end of active local interest by Webbs Crystal Glass, as BTH assumed direct control of the Hatton factory in 1921, taking a two-year lease, which would imply that from then onwards production was solely for their needs. Mr A Hill was appointed as Manager, from the wire drawing section at Rugby. Charles Tod had probably left in 1919 when he resigned as a director of Corbett & Co Ltd.

• The 1921 Census of England & Wales, released to the public in January 2022, has added considerably to the otherwise scanty information on this period in the factory's history. The Occupation/Employer details in the individual household Census Returns allow a full employee listing to be constructed for the

Scropton Lane Glassworks, as well as for the other major industrial concerns that formed the backbone of employment in Hatton, Tutbury and some of the surrounding villages.

80 local people gave their employer's name and place of work as Webbs Crystal Glass Company Ltd of Scropton Lane (or various less precise variations thereof). A detailed listing is given in Appendix G. As a comparison, 45 were working at the adjoining Tutbury/Record Engineering, 307 at nearby Nestlé's condensed milk factory, 60 at the Plaster Mill across the river, 160 at the Gypsum mines and processing plant at Fauld, 95 on the local Railway system, and 109 at Thomas Webb & Corbett Ltd's Glassworks in Ludgate Street, Tutbury. (The fact that the two glassworks at this time were both "Webbs", though totally unconnected, adds to the confusion between them that has been noted earlier.)

Half of the Scropton Lane glassworkers lived in Tutbury and made their way down over the river bridge every day. The rest were largely Hatton residents plus a handful from Rolleston and Scropton villages. About a dozen had their birthplace far afield, but the great majority were born locally. 68 were males, 12 females or, to be more precise, girls. In describing their occupations, the product references are all to "Bulbs":

      Bulb Maker
      Bulb Blower
      Bulb Gatherer
      Bulb Machine Attendant
      Bulb Packer
      Bulb Wrapper

No-one calls themselves a Cutter, indicating that traditional decorated tableware manufacture had finished. That's not to say that some of the Blowers couldn't turn their hands occasionally to some of the specialities and peculiarities mentioned earlier.

The thing that really stands out is the employees' youthfulness – 32 were teenagers (though the term was rarely in use up to that time), and a further 23 were in their twenties. This partly reflects that much of the work was unskilled or semi-skilled. Of the craftsmen pictured with Corbett in 1910, only five appear to survived – William Pavey, still blowing; George Cresswell still packing; former Cutters Joe Siddalls and Charlie Marshall, one pot-making, the other an Examiner; and it's good to see historian Frank Pegg progressing – formerly a Fitter, but now Works Foreman.

The known management team around that time, Mr Hill and Walter Reynolds, have not yet been located on the local Census. But a Charles Shann, aged 41, originally from Wolverhampton, now living with his family in Castle Street, Tutbury, describes himself as Manager of Webbs Crystal Glassworks. The 1921 Census is Shann's first appearance in the area and nothing further is known of him at present, though interestingly his three-year-old daughter had been born in Pittsburg, USA.

Besides Frank Pegg, the second tier of supervisors included Walter Duncan as Building Foreman and Lizzie Eaton, the Lamp Room Forewoman, no doubt with her hands full keeping her girls' minds on their work

It's easy to imagine what clocking on and clocking off time must have been like for the near two hundred Scropton Lane and Nestles workers living in Tutbury – rushing down Bridge Street and Station Road bleary-eyed to beat the breakfast-time hooter; and then perhaps lingering to socialise on the Dove Bridge at the end of the long day.

The Census was taken in June 1921 when the country was in the grip of a national Mineworkers' Strike. Whilst only limited support action was taken by other Unions, the shortage of coal supplies led to widespread closures in other industries, with over two million people unemployed as a result. More than half of the Ludgate Street Webb Corbett employees noted on their Census Returns that they were "out of work" at the time – but none of the Scropton Lane workers did. Some of the Webb Corbett workers specifically add that their idleness was due to a strike, though it's not clear if that was positive sympathy strike action on their part, or the knock-on effect of supply shortages. If the latter, it's feasible that Hatton's light bulb production had a higher priority in the government's allocation of limited coal stocks than Tutbury's manufacture of fancy tableware.

• On a lighter note, a year later, here are some familiar names:

British Thomson Houston Co., Ltd.

WINNERS OF THE TUTBURY & DISTRICT INTER-WORKS FOOTBALL COMPETITION, 1922.

A. E. HILL,   H. McGUINNESS,   H. W. JENNINGS,   T. SHILTON,   W. REYNOLDS,
S. WOOD,   T. TIMMINS,   G. WOOLLEY.
S WARD

Figure 29 – BTH, Trophy Winners 1922

118

Mr Hill, the Factory Manager, and Walter Reynolds, clearly still surviving as a loyal Number Two. And Harry McGuinness, Tommy Timmins and George Woolley, the next generation on from their namesakes who figured in earlier chapters. Between BTH, Webb Corbett, and probably Nestles, the Plaster Mill, the Fauld Mine, Record Engineering and maybe others, the Tutbury & District Inter-Works Football Competition (six a side?) of 1922 was no doubt a keenly contested affair. This time the Bottom Shop came out on top.

• BTH opened a major new facility in Chesterfield towards the end of 1923. All the Hatton production was switched there, together with those key employees who wanted to move (including Frank Pegg). The Scropton Lane factory ceased operations in 1924. There was a workforce of 110 at the time of closure, a major employment blow to the local community. It remained as a BTH store until 1928 with Charlie Marshall, an old RCGW employee, leading a lonely existence as Caretaker. Described on a 1937 O.S. map as "Royal Castle Glassworks (disused)", it then lay empty, still in the ownership of Webbs Crystal Glass, until 1939 when it was requisitioned by the War Department for storage purposes for the duration of the Second World War.

* * * * *

7.   1946-1984   Trent Valley Glassworks

Note: This Chapter is deliberately brief, is reliant largely on previously published material from other sources which the authors are grateful to acknowledge, and does not claim to reflect any newly-discovered sources or original research on their part. There is a much fuller story of Trent Valley Glassworks, particularly on the shop-floor, that could be better told than by the present writers. We hope that those with first-hand knowledge of the factory during their working lives might be able to do so.

The final era of glassmaking in Hatton, and the only one to remain in living memory today, began in 1946. Some authoritative oral and written history has survived, unlike the patchy records of some of the earlier ventures in Scropton Lane.

• The story of Trent Valley Glassworks is told very succinctly in the words of the 1984 booklet "The Hatton Glassmakers". Though unattributed, the publication is the work of Mr Harry Shaw, who was at TVGW for almost the entirety of its life, and to whom we are grateful for what is produced below:

"Mr. W[illiam] Bennett, the founder of Glastics Ltd., had spent a lifetime in the glass trade with the International Bottle Co., but had retired at the end of 1939. During the war years he decided that he would start a business for his two sons when they were released from the forces. So on 5th June 1944 Glastics Ltd. was formed as a merchant company dealing in glass and plastics.

However, Mr Bennett found it impossible to obtain supplies of glassware, so he decided to look into the possibility of buying an existing glassworks or of building a new one. After making many enquiries from friends in the glass trade, he contacted Mr Teisen who told him of the factory at Hatton; further he advised Mr Bennett that it should be possible to get it back into production without too much expense. Following lengthy negotiations with Webbs Crystal Glass Co, the factory was purchased for £7,000.

After visiting the factory, he wrote to one of his sons saying "The factory is situated at Tutbury about five miles from Burton-on-Trent, the country is very pretty being in the Trent Valley - the river running just near the factory". In another letter he wrote, "I called at the labour exchanges at both Derby and Burton on Trent. We come under Derby as the factory is in Hatton just over the river Trent which separates the two counties of Derbyshire and Staffordshire." The founder's poor geography resulted in the works being called "Trent Valley Glassworks" and not "Dove Valley Glassworks".

Figure 30 – 1946: Dereliction outside

Figure 31 – 1946: Dereliction inside

Having acquired the works, nothing could be done until the Army could be persuaded to move out, and this took considerable effort as it was necessary to deal with several Ministries. It was towards the end of 1946 when the works was at last released.

Before production started, the old No1 8-pot Furnace had to be repaired. The only other major work necessary was the building of a new Lehr which was gas fired. In order to avoid unnecessary expense, second hand equipment and glass machines were bought, some from Ronald Gale (Key Glassworks). Moulds were supplied by Armytage Bros and Johnson Radley. In later years as the factory expanded and more machines were required, these were bought from glassworks which had closed or ceased semi-automatic production.

A small staff was recruited, some with the required skills of semi-automatic bottle making - two of these were from Jackson Bros in Yorkshire. It was in March 1947 that production of bottles started with a total staff of 20 - production of pressware followed very shortly; this consisted mainly of 4" blue Sugar Liners for Western Glass who had supplied their own moulds early in 1947 as they were desperate for supplies. By the end of 1947, six machines were working.

The total weekly wages amounted to about £200. At that time the hourly rate for a skilled glassmaker was 2/9d (14p) and for a female sorter 1/4d (6p). Shortly after the works started, a three-shift (8 hours) operation was put into place. The week started at 10.00 pm on Sunday and finished at 6.00 pm on a Saturday - a 48-hour week. Often overtime was worked on a Sunday morning.

● It was not long before demands could not be met, so plans were made for expansion. A new 10 pot furnace was built by Teisen and this went into production in July 1950 in place of the old 8 pot furnace - in effect this gave an increase of 25% in capacity. It was also possible to increase pot sizes from 10 cwt to 12 cwt. which gave an additional increase in melting capacity." This was an early milestone, celebrated in a Burton Daily Mail front page photograph and report:

**"FINE GLASSWARE FROM ONCE DERELICT FACTORY.
HATTON ENTERPRISE.
NEW MELTING FURNACE WILL DOUBLE FIRM'S OUTPUT.**

Started in 1946, in a factory once derelict, the Trent Valley Glass Works at Hatton has made great strides, with demand for its products exceeding supply.

Yesterday saw another step forward in the life of the firm, when Mr W Bennett, the founder, inspected a flawless perfume flask, the first product of a new glass-melting furnace, calculated to double the firm's *output. From within the ageing walls of a once derelict 19th century factory at Hatton comes some of the finest glassware of Britain.*

Figure 32 – Some Key People at Trent Valley in 1950

Back row: P Bagnall, WH Bennett, W Bennett, R Layden, G Tunnicliffe, J Stubley. Front row: Miss B Smith, Mrs W Bennett, Mrs G Tunnicliffe, Mrs R Leyden, Miss B Redfern, J Clark.

Until yesterday the products of these Hatton craftsmen were fashioned from a glass-melting furnace that had, by all estimates, outlived its life years ago. Yet such was the reputation of the skill and artistry of the Trent Valley glassworkers, achieved in no more than three years, that orders exceeded output. Even by working night and day they could not satisfy the demand. Although built within crumbling walls, the new furnace is but a first step in the founder's dream of a fresh era in Hatton's ancient industry. New factory walls will eventually radiate from the furnace, out over the old site, to make the Trent Valley Glassworks among the latest and most efficient in the country."

Meanwhile the old 8-pot No.1 furnace was repaired and enlarged to a 10-pot furnace and brought into production in March 1952 giving a total of 20 pots. A second lehr was also built at this time.

- "The Hatton Glassmakers" continues: *"On 6th August 1957 the works suffered a serious flood following a very heavy storm, the whole of the factory area was under water. After the floods subsided it was possible to patch the recuperators on No.1 furnace and start production on 25th August. The recuperators on No.2 furnace had to be replaced and production was not started until 22nd September.*

On 7th December 1960 Hatton suffered from a further flood but, with the experience of the 1957 flood, various precautions had been taken to limit the effect of flooding. As a result of this, No.2 furnace was back in production as soon as the floods subsided and water around the recuperators was pumped out; that was within a few days. No 1 furnace was given a major repair which in any case was nearly due.

On the question of flooding, it is interesting to note that about half way between Hatton and Scropton there is a ridge which runs from the railway embankment, through the adjacent field and across the road. Apparently, this ridge was built to stop flood water from Scropton reaching Hatton. It is said that, at times of flooding, fighting used to take place between the inhabitants of Scropton and the Hatton glassmakers as the latter tried to stop the former destroying the ridge."

These floods, particularly the first, were dramatic affairs given the combination of the water and the furnace fires. Tutbury Museum holds internal management reports written in their aftermath, and extracts from these are given in Appendix H.

Figures 33/34 - Station Rd and Trent Valley's Yard under water

126

• The next expansion at the works took place in 1964. By this time there was a demand for larger articles especially in White Flint; it was decided that a small tank furnace was required. A new shop was built for a 4-ton oil fired tank which was in production in August 1964.

At the same time, a new office block was built at the front of the works. This time the Derby Evening Telegraph reported on the progress:

"LARGE EXTENSION TO HATTON GLASSWORKS

An extension to the Trent Valley Glassworks, Hatton, which has now been completed, will increase production by about a half.

Covering an area of 10,000 square feet, the extension has been constructed to meet the increased demand for the company's products - glass containers, extensively used by chemists and perfumers.

It includes housing for an oil-fired furnace to supplement the two coal-fired furnaces. A prefabricated chimney for the extension is now operating ...

A new office block has also been constructed, and mechanisation of the warehouse and handling is being undertaken.

Mr W H Bennett, managing director, Trent Valley Glassworks, told the Telegraph that the present number of employees, 180, would be increased by about 35 when the extension was in full production and when the necessary training had been carried out. All the labour is recruited from within a radius of five or six miles of the works."

Figure 35 - Modern Furnaces

Figure 36 - Modern Offices

Up to 1964, production had been mainly for bottles for the cosmetic and medical trades, and pressing for the mounting trade in Birmingham. The new increased capacity for white flint glass enabled production to start of well and bulkhead glasses when Pilkingtons and Sowerby Ellison ceased production of these lines.

Over the following years the furnaces were progressively switched from coal-fired to oil to natural gas, with consequent improvements in performance, cost and environmental impact.

- In the 1970s the factory suffered two serious fires.

Figure 37 – 1971 Fire

The story is picked up in "The Hatton Glassmakers": *"The first was on Saturday 7th July 1971 and affected the pot shop. The owner of the cottage next to the works had a bonfire in his garden; this spread* *to the pot shop and the wooden walls and roof were quickly ablaze.*

Although the shell of the building was destroyed, there was no damage to the furnace and lehrs. Thanks to a great effort by all concerned in clearing up and carrying out essential repairs, limited production started on the following Monday morning. A temporary roof was erected and so repairs to the building were carried out without interruption to production.

The second fire occurred on 14th March 1977 in the tank shop - the cause of this was never discovered. Considerable damage was done to packaging etc., but not to essential equipment; there was not a long interruption to production.

Figure 38 - 1977 Aftermath

Press cuttings reporting on the two fires can be found in the Museum's archives (refs GL277 and GL278j). Also to be found there is a lengthy unpublished paper by Aubrey Bailey, the manuscript text of what appears to be a slide presentation entitled "The Manufacture of Glass Containers" (GL291). It is undated, but is probably from about 1970. It gives a detailed description of the production processes across the many departments and conveys the impression of a still relatively buoyant business.

Figure 39 - Trent Valley Glassware

• "The Hatton Glassmakers" takes up the story from there: *"Since the early days of 1947 the works had melted a wide range of glasses; white flint (soda lime or clear) neutral w/f, amber, white opal and dark blue. Later this range was increased and other colours included -*

green, coloured opals, ruby, yellow and various special colours required by customers...

In the 1970s, conditions in the industry became more difficult. Although new markets were found - lighting glass, paperweights, industrial pressing, vehicle lenses etc. - the general level of business declined. The very deep recession in the early 1980's resulted in a serious shortage of work; production had to be reduced and furnaces let out.

The situation in the semi-automatic section was more serious because of the high labour content of costs. Wages had risen dramatically: in 1970 an average skilled glassmaker would earn about £30 per week. By 1980 this had risen to £100. The result was that a semi-automatic bottle would cost around five times that for a similar fully automatic; few customers would pay these prices. Further, the quality of the automatic production was very good and often better than semi-automatic quality. The modern automatic I.S. machine was also able to produce very difficult shapes which in the 1940's would have been made on semi-automatic machines. The problem has not been so severe with pressware as although there are automatic works producing good quality at low prices, there are more markets where customers only require smaller quantities, too small for automatic production. There has of course also been increasing competition from plastics.

By early 1983 there was insufficient work to keep the factory going and so it was decided to close the works and transfer the remaining business to Glastics' other site at Waterstone Glassworks. Glass production ceased at the Trent Valley Glassworks on 16th July 1983."

Some processing work and office functions remained for a few months, but on 3rd February 1984 the Derby Telegraph reported:

Hatton Factory Closes

A Hatton glassworks closes today and 24 people will become redundant. In July last year all glassmaking at the Trent Valley Glassworks of Glastics Ltd, industrial glassmakers, ceased and 54 people were made redundant. Some work was transferred to another Glastics Ltd factory in Yorkshire.

But 24 employees remained in the buildings at Scropton Lane Hatton, including office workers and people processing work. But the factory finally closes its doors today, bringing to an end the company's connection with Hatton, which began in 1947. Almost all of the people who will be thrown out of work live in the immediate area of Hatton and Tutbury.

Figure 40 – With thanks to Harry Shaw

8.   Afterthoughts

Across the 19th and 20th centuries the two neighbouring villages of Hatton and Tutbury were home to an unusually varied group of significant industries, in combination on a scale rather out of proportion to the original settlements:

- An early Cotton Mill, giving employment to hundreds of first and second generation industrial workers: men, women and children alike;
- Two substantial Glassworks, one of which gained an international reputation as Webb Corbett for the quality of its crystal tableware and the other, in Scropton Lane, which produced a wide array of different glassware;
- Two Alabaster/Gypsum Mines with related plaster processing facilities, once in the former Cotton Mill and, still active up to the present day, at the Fauld mine site;
- A series of Engineering businesses, culminating in Claytons Equipment which served a worldwide market for specialist locomotives;
- A large-scale condensed milk and later coffee-processing plant under the famous Nestlé brand, still flourishing and expanding today.

If one considers the many other villages in a several-mile radius, there are no parallels whatsoever. To the north, beyond the "Salt Box" junction and the turnpike road, was an unchanging pattern of isolated agricultural settlements rising to the Peak District foothills. To the south lay the empty estate lands of Needwood Forest. Eastwards and westwards along the Dove Valley, apart from other relatively short-lived dairies, nothing of commercial significance could be found until one reached the wider East Midlands river system - the Trent, the Derwent and the Churnet - in Burton-on-Trent, Derby and Uttoxeter.

So what were the catalysts for these industries to set up here? Hatton, as has been explained, barely existed for official purposes until the latter 19th century. Tutbury had been a militarily and politically significant stronghold and market town in medieval times, but those days were long gone and by the early 1800's it had deteriorated in status to little more than a large village of somewhat ill repute, albeit with a lot of history, a fine Georgian High Street housing a good number of middle-class families, and a well-patronised stagecoach posting inn.

The Cotton Mill came first around 1781 (after an earlier small industrial building, purportedly an 18th century Silk Mill, of which little is known), with water-power from the diverted River Dove as an obvious local resource, but needing a large labour force that had to be built up from scratch. The Ludgate Street Glassworks was next in 1810 - seemingly out of thin air, with no local raw materials, no local skilled labour, and no local manufacturing or managerial expertise; though recent research by the authors provides evidence of the Jackson family's presence in the glass merchanting trade in the USA as a likely initiative for the establishment of the factory in their home village of Tutbury.

The arrival of the North Staffordshire Railway then intervened in 1846, probably decisively. "Tutbury Station" became a locally important transport intersection, linking the railway, the main road (later the A50, now the A511) and its River Dove crossing. Through the Station raw materials came in, new employees arrived and finished goods departed from the growing industrial base. The railway provided significant employment in itself as well, reflected in the large number of railway workers living locally. Tutbury acted as the most important staging point along the 20-mile stretch of line from Derby to Uttoxeter, with an additional link to Burton-on-Trent.

Figure 41 - Tutbury Station, with the Glassworks in the far distance

Industrial development then logically followed on some of the flat agricultural land immediately north of the railway. The New (later Royal Castle) Glassworks had started after 1863 in New Scropton Lane. At the turn of the century the Photo Decorated Tile Works operated for a short period on an adjoining site, followed by the also brief episode of the Anchor & Cross Bottle Works. Technical support for the automated Anchor & Cross facilities was the work of the Trades Progress Company, which established its own base simultaneously in Scropton Lane. Engineering services continued to be provided from this site into the 1920's under the guise of the Tutbury Engineering Company and then the Record Engineering Company, re-emerging successfully after WW2 as Clayton Equipment. The milk factory was established in New Marston Lane in 1901 by the Anglo-Swiss Condensed Milk Company, which merged in 1905 with Nestlé. Later short-lived activities in the period up to WW2 in the area close to the station included the Dudley Sawmill and a flax drying process operated by Ratcliffe & Goodall Food Supplies. This is all cumulative evidence of the build-up of a favourable industrial environment, with suitable building land, good transport links and a flexible semi-skilled workforce.

Meanwhile the gypsum and alabaster measures at Fauld, exploited since at least the earliest medieval times, had seen an expansion of activity with the new drift mines of Peter Ford and J C Staton in the late 1800's, directed to the production of various forms of plaster. Cotton Spinning had by then come to an end at the Tutbury Mill and Henry Newton acquired the Mill and converted it to plaster production for the output from Staton's mine.

The subject of this study has been just one of these many ventures, the second of the Glassworks, situated in Scropton Lane, Hatton. But for anyone living in the locality in the past century, the differing industries formed something of an inter-related whole, giving identity and character to the place where you lived. And though there might supposedly be occasional hostilities between local youths from opposite sides of the river, life in the two villages was closely intertwined. You might spend all your days as a Glass Blower in Ludgate Street, but your brother was working at the "Bottom Shop", your wife had a part-time job "down Nestle's", the lad next door had been taken on as an apprentice at Claytons, and the old guy over the road had managed to get out from underground "when the Dump went up" in 1944 at Fauld. *(Both of the authors' fathers were Webb Corbett Cutters who married girls from Hatton families.)*

Many major industrial centres in the country derived their identity historically from a single dominant industry, be it coal-mining, shipbuilding, textile manufacture, metal-bashing, pottery, dockyards, fishing, etc, etc. For our two villages, it was rather a multiplicity of very differing businesses. And for our young men there wasn't just a single

137

choice of "down the pit" or "off to sea", but a wider set of options when entering the world of work and often at later stages in their working lives. For our women as well, the local firms offered a good range of employment opportunities, not always found elsewhere.

At none of these workplaces was life easy - underground at Fauld; choking in the plaster mill; six hours on, twice a day, in front of the glassworks furnace; standing all day, with wet hands, rough cutting glass in a hovel in Ludgate Street; mind-numbing hours for the unskilled. Nestle's sounded pleasanter, but perhaps the smell became a bit much at times...? Health & Safety hadn't been invented; welfare provision was minimal. Pay rates were probably fairly comparable between the different workplaces, and certainly modest - it is said that in more recent times, to keep a lid on wages, there were unwritten agreements between the various firms not to poach labour from each other though, as has been seen, wholesale defections from Tutbury to Hatton Glassworks were critical in establishing the latter on three occasions.

To concentrate finally on the Hatton Glassworks, we now have some evidence to answer the question as to how the Glassworks came to Hatton, and how it kept on re-inventing itself. There was an attractive site with good transport links and an increasing supply of labour of varied skill levels. But what stands out most clearly from the story as the constant catalyst for what happened is enterprise - the ambition, drive and ingenuity of a series of individual men. Five contrasting entrepreneurs who each, with family members, took on the challenge of building a business from scratch, on the same repeatedly derelict site, assembling a skilled workforce, innovating products and processes, pushing for sales, flourishing for a time perhaps, but all ultimately beaten by market forces lining up against them and the relentless churn of commercial life:

William Alexander Sivewright, idealistic and diplomatic, sober and religious, energetic and tireless, but ultimately perhaps naive;

John Thomas Haden Richardson, confident and determined, inventive and innovative, equally energetic, but at times rash;

Vincent McIntyre, full of North American drive and optimism, genial and eloquent, equally energetic, but soon off to pastures new;

George Harry Corbett, charming and persuasive, forceful and resourceful, equally energetic, but too often pushing his luck;

William Bennett and his sons William H and John, whom it would be presumptuous of us to characterise, but who appear to have been decent employers of a workforce many of whom look back on their time at Trent Valley Glassworks with a good deal of affection and pride.

* * * * *

9.   Notes, Sources and Acknowledgements

This book has been written primarily as a story, and there has been no intention to exhaustively reference every statement. Where practicable, specific information sources have been indicated within the body of the text. The general sources of information are listed and described below.

Unless stated, illustrations are taken from the collection of photographs and documents held by Tutbury Museum. Original sources for all have been acknowledged where known and permissions sought. A full listing of illustrations and their provenance is given at the end of this section.

• **Archives of Tutbury Museum**. The research in this book was originally stimulated by documentation much of which had been deposited with the Museum after the closure of Trent Valley Glassworks in 1984. The writing of the book has been a process of substantially adding to, refining, consolidating (and in some cases correcting) the information contained. The most valuable elements within these early sources have been:

♦ "The Hatton Glassmakers", an unattributed booklet produced in 1984, the work of Mr Harry Shaw of Trent Valley Glassworks. It pulls together what was a then fragmentary history of the earlier Hatton Glassworks, including the fruits of the researches of Mr WH Bennett, together with a fuller narrative of the story of Trent Valley Glassworks, which forms the basis of Chapter 7.
♦ "The Manufacture of Glass Containers", the unpublished text of a talk prepared by local historian and Museum founder Aubrey Bailey, which included some general history of glass and an outline of the early years of glassmaking in Hatton, as well as an extensive description of the operating departments in Trent Valley's time. It is

unclear whether it was intended as a slide presentation or a documentary film.

♦ Internal Trent Valley management reports on the floods suffered by the factory in 1957 and 1960, reproduced in Appendix I.

♦ Correspondence of Mr WH Bennett with former glassworkers in Hatton and Kent, Wilfred Woolley, Percy Farrow and Frank Pegg.

♦ Miscellaneous newspaper cuttings of events such as the Royal Visit of 1899, the opening of the Anchor & Cross Bottle Works in 1905, and the Trent Valley Glassworks fires of 1971 and 1977.

♦ A photographic archive of the local glassworks from the late 1890's up to the present day, of which the most illustrative examples have been incorporated into the narrative.

The principal additional resources that have subsequently been identified and utilised are:

• **The Flint Glass Makers' Magazine**, the quarterly journal of the glassblowers' trade union, the Flint Glass Makers' Friendly Society, of which an almost complete set for the period 1850 to 1903 is held by the Modern Records Centre of the University of Warwick, under reference MSS/YG/F/4/1. It provides a rich source of information on trade union history in general, on the issues and conditions that prevailed in the glassmaking industry in particular, and for membership details relating to the Hatton and Tutbury factories contained in the District's quarterly financial returns. The quarterly returns include data on membership numbers and the names of men receiving pension, unemployment, sickness and death benefits, or in arrears with subscriptions. The narrative section of the Journals contains editorials, reports on industrial disputes, articles on industry issues, readers' letters and occasional items of lighter relief. The FGMM is the most important source of "new" research information for Chapter 2 and, particularly, Chapter 3.

- **Companies House filings** held by The National Archives, Kew, for:
  - Corbett & Company Ltd, ref BT31/20010/115802 and BT34/3657/115802;
  - The Anchor & Cross Bottle Works Syndicate Ltd, ref BT/31/10722/81268;
  - The New Anchor & Cross Bottle Works Syndicate Ltd, ref BT/31/11022/83768;
  - The Photo Decorated Tile Company Ltd, ref BT/31/7440/52857;
  - The Trades Progress Company Ltd, ref BT31/16525/67975;
  - The New Trades Progress Company Ltd, ref BT31/11238/85842.

Companies House records from that era are very far from complete. They may include Formation and Prospectus documents, Share Issue details, Registered Addresses, and Director/Shareholder lists or changes. There is rarely financial information such as would be expected in a modern Annual Report & Accounts. Such documents as survive on file have been relied on extensively in Chapters 4 and 5, and Appendices C and D.

(Alexander Sivewright & Son and JTH Richardson & Sons were unincorporated partnerships, and as such were not subject to Company filing requirements. Trent Valley Glassworks was a division of Glastics Ltd, and not a limited company in its own right.)

Though by its nature often dry and technical, Companies House data provides some precision about dates, finances, relationships and motivations that is often lacking in more informal sources, and is relied upon extensively in this study.

- **National and regional newspaper reports**, now increasingly available and searchable on-line from various sources. Our local area is particularly fortunate with the archive of Burton-on-Trent and Derby newspapers assembled by the Magic Attic in Swadlincote, Derbyshire, which have added significantly to this story; We are very grateful to the Magic Attic for the material and advice they have provided for the production of this book.

• **Modern family history research resources,** which offer today's local historian a solid underpinning of personal details of former local inhabitants that were not so readily available to earlier writers. For the Tutbury area, extensive use has been made of the meticulous transcriptions of local records by Robert and Jeanne Minchin on behalf of Tutbury Museum, accessible and searchable via its "Superlist" database. These records include the 10-yearly Censuses from 1841 to 1921, parish registers of baptisms, marriages and burials, graveyard mapping, directories and electoral rolls. The commercial family history databases, Ancestry.co.uk and findmypast.co.uk have been used as the starting point for similar records outside of the Tutbury area, plus civil registrations of births, marriages and deaths.

• **Large scale Ordnance Survey and other maps of the Hatton area.** Maps extracts used in this book are reproduced in accordance with the copyright guidelines of the Ordnance Survey and, where accessed via the National Library of Scotland website, in accordance with the definition of non-commercial use for material with a Creative Commons Attribution. The National Library of Scotland's on-line archive is an excellent access point to many old O.S. maps. Early Tithe Maps are held by local County Records Offices. A copy and analysis of the 1840 Tutbury Tithe Map and Apportionment is held by Tutbury Museum. Interpretation of old maps is not always straightforward and Mr Tony Beresford has provided valuable advice, as well as other information on Hatton, its residents and railways.

• **Commercial Trade Directories**, held variously by the William Salt Library, Stafford and Tutbury Museum, or accessed via www.forebears.co.uk .

● **Personal testimony and documentation from:**
- Dianne and Alan Purvis, a New Zealand descendant of William Alexander Sivewright;
- Ron Dent, a descendant of George Harry Corbett;
- Harry Shaw, formerly of Trent Valley Glassworks;
- Jack Mear, formerly of Trent Valley Glassworks;
- Francis Toye;
- Chris Key, long-time Editor of the Hatton News;
- Mary Pollard, Park Hill House, Tutbury.

● **Wikipedia** has been the prime starting point for general information on miscellaneous subjects including James Eadie, the Isle of Sheppey, Stanley Jenkinson, British Thomson-Houston, Webb's Crystal Glass, Clarence Hatry, and the 1921 Miners' Strike.

Acknowledgement is also made to:
● Stoke-on Trent Archives: Thomas Webb & Corbett Ltd Letter Book 1910, reference SD1705/WC/Crate 2/1. This contains correspondence with references to G H Corbett's departure from the company (Chapter 5).
● Tutbury Book of Remembrance, Volume 1, 2nd Edition – 2014, by Jane and Rick Nuth, used as the source for casualties of World War 1 in the local area (Chapter 5).
● Jason Ellis, "Glassmakers of Stourbridge and Dudley, 1612-2002: A biographical history of a once great industry". A compendious reference work, this has provided valuable background data on a number of the West Midlands glassmaking families with connections to the subject of this book – the Richardson, Webb, Corbett and Guest families.
● Ian Dury and the Glasshouse Heritage Centre, Stourbridge.

Illustration Sources:

Figure

1	National Library of Scotland
2	Derived from Figure 1
3	Tutbury Museum, ref GL398
4	The National Archives, ref COPY 1/51/137
5	Tutbury Museum, ref GL118, donation of TVGW management
6	Tutbury Museum, ref GL120, donation of TVGW management
7	Tutbury Museum, ref GL402, donation of Dianne and Alan Purvis
8	The Pottery and Glass Trades Journal October 1879
9	Tutbury Museum, ref GL399, donation of Mr Ron Dent
10	National Library of Scotland
11	Ian Dury, Glasshouse Heritage Centre
12	Tutbury Museum, ref GL357, donation of Angela Gove
13	Tutbury Museum, ref GL122
14	Derived from Figure 13
15	"Tutbury Cricket Club 1872-1972"
16	Tutbury Museum, ref GL152
17	Author's photograph
18	Tutbury Museum, ref GL239
19	By permission of the Centre for Photographic Conservation
20	National Library of Scotland
21	Journal of The Society of Glass Technology 1922
22	Tutbury Museum, ref GL400
23	Tutbury Museum, ref GL102, donation of Charles Crossley
24	Tutbury Museum, ref GL107-2, donation of Charles Crossley
25	Tutbury Museum, ref GL108, donation of Charles Crossley
26	Mr Ron Dent
27	Tutbury Museum, ref GL36
28	Tutbury Museum, ref GL99
29	Tutbury Museum, ref TP05
30	Tutbury Museum, ref GL116, donation of TVGW management
31	Tutbury Museum, ref GL119, donation of TVGW management
32	Tutbury Museum, ref GL150ac, donation of TVGW management
33	Tutbury Museum, ref GL150ag, donation of TVGW management
34	Tutbury Museum, ref GL121, donation of TVGW management
35	Tutbury Museum, ref GL124, donation of TVGW management
36	Tutbury Museum, ref GL117, donation of TVGW management
37	Tutbury Museum, ref GL114, donation of TVGW management
38	Tutbury Museum, ref GL112, donation of TVGW management

39 Tutbury Museum, ref GL138, donation of TVGW management
40 Tutbury Museum, ref GL139, donation of TVGW management
41 Author's collection
42 Modern Records Centre, University of Warwick, ref MSS.126/YG/F/1/7
43 Tutbury Museum, ref VP86
44 Tutbury Museum, ref TP44
45 The National Archives, ref BT31/16525/67975
46 The National Archives, ref BT31/11238/85842
47 Tutbury Museum ref GL102, donation of Charles Crossley
48 Tutbury Museum ref GL104-2, donation of Charles Crossley

10. Appendices:

A. JTH Richardson's Glass-breaking Dispute 1881

Report from The Flint Glass Makers' Magazine. (Reproduced by permission of the Modern Records Centre, University of Warwick, ref MSS/YG/F/4/1/7)

THE

flint Glass Makers' Magazine.

NEW SERIES.

| No 19.] | *NOVEMBER,* 1881. | [*Vol 6.* |

THE TUTBURY TRIAL CASE ON CUSTOM.

FELLOW WORKMEN,—

We promised in our last report to print a record of the Trial with Mr. Richardson, of Tutbury, and stated that it would prove one of the most interesting in the history of our Trade.

Some time ago the District Secretary forwarded us a report of the Tutbury District Meeting, held concerning the cruel manner in which the Employer was treating the men, and the large amount of work he was continually taking off them ; work that he called bad : it mattered not if it was "cordy," or "stony," or faulty in manipulation. This, with good and passable work, was taken and placed in a warehouse for sale. Some weeks it was two moves, other weeks five moves, and in some cases it had reached as much as eight moves to the chairs affected, and not one single penny was allowed for it. This, as our readers will be aware, became so intolerable that the men could stand it no longer, and we must say that when we come to look into the case, we can only wonder how they stood it so long. The Secretary sent us a full report, and with it a request from the men, that we should come down and enquire into the case, and see how matters stood. Having gone down, we found what the men had said was only too true, and we at once saw Mr. Richardson upon the matter, and told him that the Executive of the Trade did not acknowledge the

A

147

right of men's work being taken from them, and put on one side to be sold, either for thirds or seconds, the men not being paid one single fraction for it. We further said that he would have to work as other respectable manufacturers did, and to observe what had always been the custom long before he was in the Trade, namely, to break the work down. The Deputation told him in plain terms that if they worked for him they should break it down, and then he could please himself what course he might think proper to take. He said that he should not allow anyone to break his work down, but he was reminded that although he placed the picked-out work in the warehouse, that it was only a portion of his property, and he had no right to dispose of it without paying the men who had spent their labour upon the articles, which was of greater importance than his material. So long as custom was acknowledged both by masters and men, what right had he to sell the work, a portion of which belonged to the men?

We ask, through the pages of the Magazine, what right had Mr. Richardson to usurp that principle which is and always will be one of the most sacred to the Glassworker? and we feel proud to say that we do not have many cases of this unmanly character exhibited towards our members. I know of nothing so inhuman or selfish in man as a manufacturer fighting with his capital against labour, to disarm men of what is possibly their only means of living. Can any mind conceive a more tyrannical act than to take off work and then sell it, knowing at the same time the poor workman has not been paid? Those who do acts of this kind must know that there will sure to come a day of retribution. Such a time came to the Employer at Tutbury. It was a day of humiliation before a Court of Magistrates and the public for him to acknowledge that he sold the work after taking it off the men. One of the chairs was stopped twenty-one moves in seven weeks' work. Such conduct, as our readers must think, was revolting in the highest degree to the natural feelings of the men. We know it is our duty to work, as we have no other means of living honourably, and as long as we can work we have by all law the right to be paid, and if the work has been made bad and acknowledged by our fellow workmen, then it should be destroyed, unless some arrangement between the employer and the men is made agreeable to both parties.

The Deputation argued with the Employer over and over again, but to no purpose, and we then gave him notice that at the expiration of one month, unless he complied with the custom of the Trade, we should give orders to his men to break down the work which he acknowledged was not saleable. As the time grew on towards the end of the notice, the men went to see him, and he told them that he should not comply with their wish as it was not the custom.

The District Secretary then wrote to me, and I gave him the necessary instructions to tell the men to break down the work; consequently they commenced, and a few wines were broken. Mr. Richardson then sent for a police officer, and locked up the warehouse so that the men could not get in. He then applied to the Magistrates for summonses, which were granted against six of the men. On the summonses were certain amounts claimed for damages for the seven wines that were wilfully broken.

The 30th of October was the day fixed for the hearing before the Bench, at a small village about five miles from Tutbury, called Sudbury. I was then instructed by the C.C. to get the best advocate that money could procure. We, therefore, at once, commenced to get up the brief for the Solicitor, and as there are many technical points in our Trade we thought it our duty to draw up an account of the whole case, and having submitted it to the Solicitor, he went carefully through it, and stated that there was a great amount of credit due to the Executive in producing the evidence in so comprehensive a manner. We then arranged with him as to his fee, and he undertook the case for £10 10s. with his expenses to Sudbury and back. We are pleased to report that he was a most able pleader, and defended the case with a vigour and ability to be commended, proving himself a "foeman worthy of his steel," discussing the question on points of law, and showing the Magistrates that the C.S. had given Mr. Richardson a month's notice, that according to custom the work when condemned should be broken down, which he held was the only proper course to take.

By arrangement I met the advocate at New-street (Birmingham) Station, at half-past eight on Monday morning, the 30th of

A*

October. With one of the finest mornings that nature could favour us, we started on our journey to Burton, arriving there by ten o'clock, and in a few minutes we were on the road for Sudbury. This is a delightful road, and the sun was sending out its beautiful rays as warm as if in the month of June, the birds were chirping, and all nature seemed alive, and presented the gayest aspect. Under such favourable circumstances we could not but feel much happier than if it had been a dull or wet day. We called *en route* at the Castle Inn, Tutbury, where we were joined by the men, who were in good spirits. Continuing on our way to the Court at Sudbury we met numbers of gentlemen in hunting attire, it being the first meet of the season at Lord Vernon's. At last, having arrived at the *Vernon Arms* where the Magistrates hold their Courts we found the Court crowded by persons anxious to hear this important trial. The gentlemen on the Bench were—The Hon. E. Coke and G. W. Peach, Esq. We had not to wait long before our case was called. Mr. Richardson's advocate opened the case and made an elaborate speech, asking the Magistrates for a case of wilfully destroying Mr. Richardson's property, which of course would mean sending. each member to prison. He quoted several cases under various Acts, and also trials that had taken place where men had been sent to gaol for the destruction of property. But this advocate forgot that some of that property was the workmanship of those whom he had summoned for destroying, and that the system had been carried on for years of stopping the men, and then selling the part that they had not been paid for. Instead of the men being summoned, it would have been more just to have summoned Mr. Richardson for selling the men's part, without paying them for it, and to have surcharged him back for all that he had sold of that portion which did not belong to him. Nor had he a right, according to law, to have acted as he did, as was shown by the cross-examination of our advocate. He confessed that he did sell the work placed in the warehouse as seconds. What right had he to sell the work for seconds, or even thirds, that had not been paid for, and because the men broke down the worth of 1s. 2d. condemned work, he thought that he was going to ride rough shod over them and send them to prison. Is this worthy of an Employer? Will not such action be held up to universal contempt?

Figure 42 – The Flint Glass Makers' Magazine

150

APPENDIX

B. Royal Visit by the Duchess of York 1899

Burton Chronicle report, 22nd August 1899:
"ROYAL VISIT TO TUTBURY
DUCHESS OF YORK TAKES TEA AT THE CASTLE
A HEARTY WELCOME

The intention of the Duchess of York to visit Tutbury Castle during her stay with the Hon. H J and Lady Catherine Coke at Longford Hall became known locally several days ago, but there being some doubt as to the actual date and time, a telegram was received in Tutbury on Monday stating that her Royal Highness would arrive about three o'clock that afternoon. The town was in consequence decorated for the occasion, and a large crowd assembled in the main thoroughfares, while the Tutbury Band turned out to meet her. She, however, never came and there was of course great disappointment all round. A rumour afterwards got abroad that the Duchess proposed visiting the Castle on the following day (Tuesday), and this fortunately turned out to be correct, though even up to the eleventh hour many doubted whether the Royal visit would actually take place, for not even Mr Stone, the caretaker of the Castle, had any official notification of it. Notwithstanding, however, that many people went from Tutbury to Clough Hall to participate in a local Primrose League picnic, there were many townsfolk and others from the surrounding district to witness her Royal Highness's arrival. She left Longford Hall at three o'clock, Hatton being reached three quarters of an hour later. At Hatton the Board School children lined the road facing the school, and as the carriage passed they saluted and gave three cheers for the Duchess, who gracefully bowed in acknowledgment. The weather was brilliant, and the drive was greatly enjoyed by her Highness, who arrived at Tutbury shortly before four o'clock, and alighted near the railway station, having accepted invitations on the part of Mr J T H Richardson and Mr G H Grundy to visit respectively the Royal Castle Glassworks and the Photo-Decorated Tile Co's manufactory. The Duchess was accompanied by Lady Katherine Coke, Earl and Countess Lathom, Mrs Crutchley and Mr Reginald Coke. She looked charming in a costume of plain pale grey, with black velvet belt, and wore a hat of pale straw to match, trimmed with pink wild roses and grey wings. The Royal party were received by Mr J T H Richardson...

AT THE GLASS WORKS [*This section of the Report is given in Chapter 3*]

Having spent over an hour at Mr Richardson's Works the party expressed great pleasure with all they had seen. They then went to

PHOTO-DECORATED TILE CO'S MANUFACTORY

hard by. This place has been opened but a couple of years and is, we believe, the only works of the kind in the country where highly artistic models and tiles are produced by purely photographic means. By this company's process photos of human beings, animals, rural scenes or any other objects of interest are transferred to encaustic tiles and there remain a permanent glazed picture warranted to stand the test of time. The tiles are used for ornamental decorative purposes for mansion, villa or office. The Duchess was received by Mr G H Grundy, business manager; and Mr B Alexander, the works manager, and Mr W W Evans, the outside salesman, were also present. First of all the party visited the photographic room, where Mr Martin, the firm's photographer, took an excellent portrait of the Duchess at Mr. Grundy's request, and afterwards photographed the Royal party in a group. These are to be modelled and printed on tiles to be sent to Her Royal Highness. The whole process of photo-modelling and printing was viewed with the keenest interest. Amongst the photo-printed tiles and panels to which special attention was directed were those bearing subjects such as Landseer's "Maid and the magpipe" [sic], "Haddon Hall", "Windsor Castle", "Tutbury Castle", "Dickens", "Burns", and a three-tiled panel called "Aurore", from a celebrated statue at the Louvre in Paris. On other tiles and panels were depicted "the old Norman staircase at Canterbury" and "Low tide at Woodbridge". Samples of photo-printing from air-brush work were also shown, the visitors being particularly struck with the perfect reproduction of the half-tones. The glazing and colour-grinding department was next visited, and it was here explained that some of the mills had to run for a week to enable the material to reach perfection. The glost kilns, each having a

152

capacity for two thousand tiles, were duly inspected, as well as other departments where much of the technical work is done. In fact the Duchess spent over an hour at the place, and said what a delightful experience her visit to that and the adjoining works had been. She was greatly surprised at the beauty of the tiles and panels, and was assured that the subjects photographed thereon and glazed were absolutely permanent records which will never fade. Before leaving, Her Royal Highness expressed her sincere thanks for the kindness and courtesy extended to her both at the glass works and the tile manufactory, the like of which she had never before seen.

AT THE CASTLE

A large crowd had been waiting in the vicinity of Tutbury station for over two hours in order to see the Duchess, and as the Royal party drove off they were heartily cheered, while the railway men fired the Royal salutes with fog signals. Although there had been no official intimation of the visit to the castle ruins many people had assembled there, including a party from Derby, in spite of the previous day's disappointment. The carriage drove up to John o' Gaunt's gateway at a quarter to six, and the Duchess who had a very cordial reception, walked across the courtyard. She first ascended the castle wall, being much impressed with the beauty of the surrounding scenery, and afterwards inspected the well and the famous dungeon. Needless to say, her presence at the historic ruins was under much happier auspices than the Royal visit to Tutbury in 1569, when the castle became the prison of Mary Queen of Scots, who was removed from Bolton Castle in Yorkshire, under the care of George, Earl of Shrewsbury, and remained here about a year and a half. Mr Stone, the caretaker, had very thoughtfully provided tea for the Royal party, and as the hour was getting late his hospitality was gratefully accepted by the distinguished visitors. Before departing the Duchess, who left about a quarter past six, expressed her thanks to Mr Stone for the kindness she had received at his hands, and said she would ever remember her visit to Tutbury as being one of the happiest days of her life. As the carriage drove off three loud cheers were accorded the Duchess who gracefully acknowledged the same, and Longford Hall was again reached about seven o'clock."

Royal Visit to Longford Hall, near Derby, Aug., 1899.
(THE SEAT OF THE HON. HENRY COKE.)

Figure 43 - The Duchess of York (front centre) at Longford Hall

154

APPENDIX

C. The Photo Decorated Tile Works in Hatton c.1900

This interesting though short-lived business, a next-door neighbour of JTH Richardson's Glassworks, first comes to prominence locally at the time of the Royal Visit of 1899. Much of the background to the enterprise is told in a Derby Telegraph article (date unknown), about George Grundy and written by journalist Peter Seddon. A copy can be found in Tutbury Museum's archives. It is a lively tale, though the information sources are not given. It appears to be based partly on the researches of Michael Swann, a local ceramic tile enthusiast under whose name a similar article appeared in the Autumn 1988 edition of "Glazed Expressions", the journal of the Tiles & Architectural Ceramics Society, and later in the "Derbyshire Life" magazine of October 2009. The technical information, derived in part from patent applications, is no doubt accurate, but unfortunately the references to the involvement of Richardson and the Royal Castle Glass Works do not readily tally with Companies House records.

The production processes that had been established in Scropton Lane by 1899 are outlined in the Burton Chronicle report of the time in Appendix B above. Mr Seddon describes how the venture originated in the hands of George Grundy and George Lingard, who together established a well-regarded print business, including retail premises in The Strand Arcade, Derby. Grundy began experimenting with the application of photographic images onto pottery. Decorative tiles were very much in Victorian fashion, and Grundy succeeded in establishing a cost-effective photo-collographic process for the decoration of tiles, where others in the industry had failed. The business took off.

The Derby Telegraph article goes on to state that at the turn of the century Grundy sold his patent to the Royal Castle Glass Works, who continued the operations *"from a corner of their premises in Scropton Lane"* under the name of The Photo-Decorated Tile Company Ltd. Fashion quickly changed however and production ceased by 1902. It is asserted that Grundy had astutely cashed in while his tiles were riding the crest of a wave, and that

Richardson's Glassworks took the financial hit from the rundown of the business. The impression given is that the tile-making was relocated to Hatton in the hands of the Glassworks and that the limited company was a creation of the Glassworks.

Companies House and other records indicate some differences in the trajectory of events. The Photo Decorated Tile Co Ltd was incorporated much earlier than the time of any RCGW involvement, on 4th June 1897 with a nominal capital of £25,000. The company was a joint enterprise between Grundy, Lingard and a Benjamin Alexander on the one hand, and an investment firm, Gold Estates of Australia Ltd (!) (The latter owed its origins to the 1893 discovery of gold in Kalgoorlie, Western Australia which, with predominantly British finance, was destined to become the most productive gold mining area in Australia. Its successor company remains today the foremost real estate developer in Western Australia. Remarkably its own website still refers to unsuccessful early diversification *"forays into other endeavours, such as copper mining in Tasmania and acquiring the patents for printing photographs directly onto tiles..."*). Simultaneously with its incorporation, The Photo Decorated Tile Co Ltd agreed to purchase from Grundy, Lingard and Alexander the photographic patents and the goodwill, plant, stock and tools of the business in Derby. In return the three received £2,000 in cash plus 19,000 fully paid shares in the new company. Grundy was appointed as Business Manager, Alexander as Photographer and Works Superintendent, and Lingard as Machinist and Collotype Plate Maker.

Share registers at the end of 1902 and 1904 show the company's shares as still held by Grundy, Lingard and Alexander, by Gold Estates and by a number of smaller investors. At the time Lingard's address was given as Oak Villas, Hatton and Alexander's as Scropton Corner, Hatton; Grundy was at 27 Duffield Road, Derby. The company was wound up in 1905 at the instigation of Gold Estates as a debenture holder. For the last years of its existence from 1900 to 1905 The Photo Decorated Tile Company Ltd was probably dormant - there is for instance a note that no AGM was held in 1904 - and the 1902 and 1904 share registers lodged at Companies House have out of date information. Most crucially, Benjamin Alexander was already dead - The National Probate Register records that Benjamin Alexander, a Works Manager of Hatton Road near Tutbury, Derbyshire [sic], died on 9th

October 1899, administration of his estate of just £128 being granted to his widow Isabella. Aged only 37, he was buried at Marston-on-Dove - just a few weeks after welcoming the Duchess of York.

There is no reference in these surviving company records to the RCGW or JTH Richardson playing any direct part in The Photo Decorated Tile Co Ltd as a company. Additionally. the impression given that the tile operation in Hatton was solely carried out from a corner of RCGW's premises does not fit with other evidence. The most graphic is the following advertising tile, from the collection of Tutbury Museum, which shows a photographic depiction of "Works, Hatton, nr Burton-on-Trent. (Tutbury Station, NSR)",

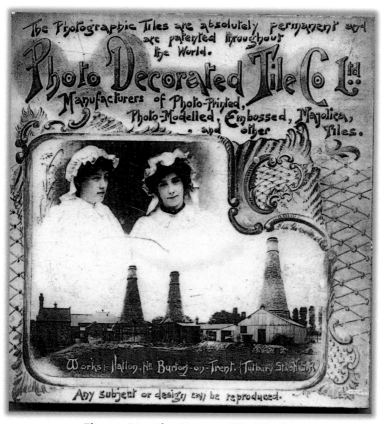

Figure 44 - The Hatton Tile Works

What is illustrated is clearly a significant operation quite separate from the Glassworks. Other evidence to support this includes:
- A substantial stand-alone Tile Works depicted and named on the 6" Ordnance Survey map of 1899, a little distance to the east of the RCGW.
- The comments of local historian Mr Peter Toye: *"I well remember during my early years at Clayton, many pieces of tile having photographs on them were found when foundations were being excavated."* (Hatton News, February 1998, Issue 69).
- The press report on the Royal Visit of 1899 describing a stand-alone manufactory of The Photo Decorated Tile Company, under the management of Grundy and Alexander.

The Works shown on the tile have three kilns/chimneys and a number of ancillary buildings. The tops of two of the RCGW chimneys can be seen in the distance, away to the west, behind a line of trees. The intervening fields were undeveloped at the time, but later became the site of the Anchor & Cross Bottle Works. Both the Tile Works and the Bottle Works were incorporated into the Engineering Works which subsequently developed on the site (see Appendix D).

Combining the stories of Mr Swann and Mr Seddon with the evidence above, the likely scenario is that Grundy and his associates Lingard and Alexander, with the investment finance of Gold Estates behind them, established the Hatton Tileworks in 1897/8 under the aegis of The Photo Decorated Tile Company Ltd, and ran it there as a management team until at least the second half of 1899. It was perhaps already running out of commercial steam by then, but the early death in October of that year of Benjamin Alexander, the key man on the shop floor, could have been a fatal blow for the business's prospects as well. JTH Richardson, either in his own name or through the RCGW, may well have acquired the patents at that time, and, in an effort to reduce costs, may indeed have ultimately moved the operation into the glassworks premises and dispensed with the remaining management team. One can see logic in Richardson looking for some diversification away from his struggling glass business. It would have been to no avail however, as the photographic tile venture fell victim to changes in technology and fashion and accompanied the RCGW on the route to closure.

But with his Glassworks in difficulty, it would be surprising if Richardson had the spare funds available to pay anything really significant for the patents. Certainly Grundy, Lingard and Alexander had partially cashed in on their innovation with the £2,000 received from Gold Estates in 1897. But how far any later costs of the business's demise fell on Richardson or on the original management team and the rest of the shareholders of The Photo Decorated Tile Co Ltd is not clear. Gold Estates' role as a debenture holder in winding the company up in 1905 indicates that they still had a financial interest.

Next door to the Richardson family in Scropton Lane on the 1901 Census lived William Mapp, an "Encaustic Tile Warehouseman". There were no other Tile workers evident in the vicinity, which indicates that by that time (April 1901) tile production had probably ceased and there was perhaps no more than a warehousing operation disposing of remaining stock, closely mirroring what had happened to the Glassworks.

George H Grundy died aged 74 at the address of his post-war theatrical and toy shop, 1 Bold Lane, Derby. His estate, administered by two of his spinster daughters, was just £175, suggesting that his later business ventures were not spectacularly successful.

But to finish on a brighter note, the focus can be turned onto the two beguiling young ladies depicted on the advertising tile. They are understood to be the Hearnden sisters from Tutbury, on the left Emma aged 18 at the turn of the century and her sister Harriet aged 17. They lived in Fishpond Lane in what must have been straitened circumstances with their widowed mother Fanny, a former Cotton Mill Hand, whose husband William, a Blacksmith's Striker, had died young in 1889. Emma married George Mear in 1901, Harriet married Albert Haynes in 1907. Both raised families locally. Emma died in 1950, Harriet in 1972. Whether the girls were employed at the Tile Works is not clear - on the 1901 Census Harriet was engaged in general domestic services and Emma had no occupation, but tile-making may already have come to an end in Scropton Lane by then and put them out of a job. Hopefully their brief modelling careers brought the two belles a little local celebrity and perhaps a bit of pin money to put towards the family budget or for their bottom drawers.

APPENDIX

D. The Trades Progress Company 1905

The Trades Progress Company Ltd ("TPC") was incorporated as a company limited by guarantee in November 1900. It was set up primarily as an investment company, to act as bankers, promoters, agents, patent holders, etc. The subscribers to the Memorandum appear a motley crew: Reginald N Hincks, Gentleman; Walter Goldschmidt, Gentleman; John Joseph MacIntyre, a Merchant of Surrey; Arthur P Mack, Gentleman; W Cobb, Gas Fitter; H Osborne, Clerk; and W G Hicks.

The first Directors were John J MacIntyre who became Managing Director describing himself also as a Contractor, Hincks who acted as Company Secretary, Walter Furze, Gentleman, who died within three years, and Vincent J MacIntyre of Hendon.

In 1901 John and Vincent McIntyre were living in Victoria Street. London in a large, confusing, cosmopolitan household, the unraveling of which is outside the scope of this study. John was aged 50, a Mechanical Engineer, an American citizen born in Canada. His son Vincent was aged 23, also a Mechanical Engineer of American citizenship. In 1892 they had been living in Niagara, New York State, with John's wife Catherine.

In December 1904 the company moved its Registered Office from London to Tutbury, with Vincent acting as Company Secretary. The Company's letterhead listed its business as "Manufacturing & Consulting Industrial Engineers; Experts in Special Machinery; Continuous Glass Tank Furnaces; Gas Producers; Continuous Glass Annealing Lehrs; Glass Pressing & Blowing Machinery; Tumbler Cap & Stopper Presses; Plans and Specifications of Modern Glass Works." Kelly's Directory indicates that the business already had a presence in the village by 1902, with Vincent McIntyre as manager, but it is not clear whether they were already on the Scropton Lane site (using the former Tile Works) by that date, nor whether their arrival had been in anticipation of their contract for the construction of the adjoining Anchor & Cross Bottle Works which eventually opened in October 1905.

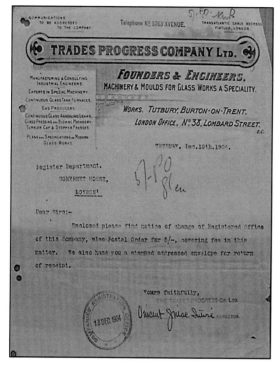

The TPC Register of Directors at the time recorded both of the McIntyres as living in Foston. They had been joined as Directors by Horace Beatson White, a Gentleman of Suffolk (quite possibly with family connections to Beatsons, the important Yorkshire glass bottle manufacturers) and John William Marwood, a Bookkeeper from Derby, appointed on 26th September 1905.

The Scropton Lane venture required funding from outside investors and, probably in order to facilitate this, it was

Figure 45 - TPC Letterhead

decided to wind up the existing company and transfer its activities into a second company, "The New Trades Progress Company Ltd" ("NTPC"). NTPC was a "normal" company limited by shares (£16,000 authorised capital), and probably more appropriate for raising finance than the peculiar structure of TPC as a company limited by guarantee. NTPC's object was to acquire as a going concern the undertaking of TPC and to act as iron founders, mechanical and consulting engineers, manufacturers of machinery, especially for glass bottles.

The NTPC balance sheet opposite, as at 1st July 1905, was attached to the acquisition agreement between the old and new companies.

From a financial perspective it appears sound enough, with the Scropton Lane Land & Buildings (apparently freehold), valued at £4,027, Plant and Machinery of £4,146, Patents, Goodwill and Securities of £2,384, and current assets of stock, work-in-progress, book debts and cash totaling £3,031. Trade and other liabilities amounted to £1,283, and £2,052 was owed to Horace Beatson White under a debenture loan.

This all equated to a net worth of £10,253, for which 10,253 £1 shares in NTPC were issued.

An engineering contractor is to a large extent only as valuable and viable as the strength of its order book. The potential of the New Trades Progress Company to progress beyond its flagship contract to build the Anchor & Cross Bottle Works was what its investors were taking a gamble on, knowingly or not.

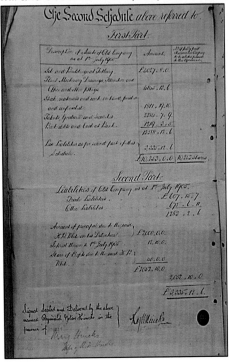

Figure 46 - NTPC Balance Sheet

The subscribers to the Memorandum this time (their signatures witnessed by W R Pye of 24 Ludgate Street, Tutbury) were:

John McIntyre, Manufacturer, of Tutbury;
William Lamont, Glassmaker, of Scropton Lane, Foston;
Vincent McIntyre, Engineer, of Tutbury;
J W Marwood, Bookkeeper, of Derby;
Harold W Brunton, Engineer, of Scropton Lane, Foston;
A E Clarke, Typist, of Derby;
Edward A Lawford, Banker's Clerk, of London.

After completion of the construction of The Anchor & Cross Works the engineering business's fortunes are at present not fully clear. We do know that trade was poor at the factory in 1906 when men were laid off. It was in operation in 1908 at the time of the molten glass incident, but was referred to as "the Tutbury Engineering Works" in the newspaper reporting. Its glass machinery activities were carried on into the 1920's under the guise of the Tutbury Engineering Company and the Record Engineering Company.

But steps to wind up the NTPC itself were commenced in July 1906. At an Extraordinary General Meeting at the company's offices in Scropton Lane on July 19th (chaired by Horace Beatson White, who as debenture holder was presumably calling the shots) it was resolved "That it has been proved to the satisfaction of the Company that the Company cannot by reason of its liabilities continue in business, and that it is advisable to wind up the same, and accordingly that the Company be wound up voluntarily under the provisions of the Companies Acts 1862-1900". Mr James J Gillespie of Newcastle upon Tyne was appointed Liquidator. No quorum was present for a final winding up meeting in January 1908, but the company was finally dissolved in May 1910. It therefore appears that around 1906 the NTPC's activities were taken over by the Tutbury Engineering Company, but whether there was any continuity of the McIntyres and other investors in either the management or financing is not known.

The McIntyres have not been located on the 1911 UK Census, and probably moved abroad again. Vincent MacIntyre is recorded as a passenger arrival in New York from Liverpool in 1907.

APPENDIX

E. Tutbury and Hatton Glassworkers living in Kent 1911

Information taken from the 1911 Census and other sources on local-born Glassworkers and their families who moved by train to the distant Isle of Sheppey in Kent in 1910 when the Anchor & Cross Bottle Works relocated their operations to the Rushenden Industrial Estate. All were born in Hatton or Tutbury unless stated otherwise.

• Annie and John Corden aged 40, a General Labourer at the Queenborough Glass Bottle Works. Boarding with them on the Isle of Sheppey were our friend Wilfred Woolley aged 23, a Ware Sorter at the Works, their nephew Charles Drury aged 16, a Machine Operator and Joseph Kirkham aged 21, a Glass Gatherer. John Corden was still in Queenborough in 1921; Wilfred Woolley remained all his life in Sheppey, as did Charles Drury.

• Thomas Hodson Walker aged 50, a Carter born in Stretton, with his wife Harriett and seven family members including sons Thomas 23, Francis 15 born Scropton and nephew Frederick Johnson 18 born Scropton, all Gatherers at the Bottle Works. It appears that the family remained and made their lives in Kent.

• Elizabeth and Thomas Shepherd aged 24, a Glass Bottle Gatherer, with two infant daughters. Walter Hawksworth aged 23, also a Gatherer, was boarding with them. Thomas Shepherd was still in Queenborough in 1921.

• William Salt aged 34 born Foston, a Gas Maker at the Glass Works, with his wife Sarah and seven young children, plus boarders Henry and William Kirkham aged 19 and 18 respectively, both Gatherers. Their later lives have not yet been traced.

• John McGuiness aged 34, a Gatherer, with his wife Clara and five children, plus two Burton lads boarding with them, George R Black 19 and Albert Dent 18, both Gatherers. Clara McGuiness remained and died in Sheppey in 1963. George Black came back home in 1912 to marry Fanny Woolley, but they appear to have returned to Sheppey, from where they maintained contact with people in Hatton into the 1970's.

• Elizabeth Bacon, a widow aged 37, is a notable case. Born into the prominent McGuiness family of Tutbury Glassblowers, her husband John Bacon had died in 1904; despite this, she upped and moved to Kent in 1910 with two young daughters and 16-year-old son Edward Bacon who became a Packer at the Queenborough Bottle Works. To make ends meet, she had five young men from the Works boarding with her - including four Tutbury-born boys, Thomas Dudley, a Sorter aged 20, Charles Compson, a Presser aged 18, Joseph Priestley, a Gatherer aged 16, and Thomas Parker, a Sorter aged 20. Elizabeth stayed on the Isle of Sheppey and died there in 1940.

• James Reginald Doohan aged 20, a Glass Blower, was boarding with a local family; he stayed on in Kent and died in 1970.

• Charles Brown aged 18 and George Harrison aged 19, both Glass Bottle Makers, were boarding with Ernie Baker, a Bottle Maker and his family who originated from Stourbridge. The boys were still in Queenborough in 1921.

• Mary and Joseph Dudley aged 24, a Foreman Sorter at the Glass Bottle Works, were sharing a house with Joseph Goring aged 24 born Hamstall Ridware, a Glass Maker, and his Tutbury-born wife Phoebe. The later lives of the Dudleys have not yet been traced. The Gorings were still in Queenborough in 1921.

• Joseph Partington aged 40, born in Tamworth, with a Derby-born wife, was a Stoker at the Glass Works. He clearly came to Kent via Hatton as his three young children were born in Foston and Scropton between 1905 and 1908. He is probably the Joseph C M Partington who died on Sheppey in 1946.

• George King aged 33 and his wife Kate, both born in Derby, were living with their two young children at Cowsted Cottages, Minster-in-Sheppey; George was an Iron Fitter and Turner in the Mould Making Room at the Glass Works; their son was born eight months previously in Sheppey, but their daughter had been born in Foston, Derbyshire two years earlier. George King, at least, was still in Sheppey in 1921.

• Lily and Thomas Brettell aged 33 born Hatton, a Glassmaker at the Bottle Works, with their two infant sons. The couple had moved around the country before 1910 and a Lily Brettell of her age died in Dudley in 1973, but it is not certain if that is where the family eventually settled.

• Sydney Stringer aged 24, a Glass Sorter at the Bottle Works, and his wife of one year, Emily, born in Church Broughton. Sydney's mother was from the ubiquitous Tutbury family of Woolleys. Visiting them was Frank Norton, a Grocer's Assistant aged 22 from Burton. Sydney later returned to East Staffordshire where he died in 1963.

• John Bridges aged 42, a Glass Blower, was lodging with a local Queenborough family, together with his 15-year-old son Harold, a Labourer. His wife Sarah and their six other children had stayed back at home in 1911 with her widowed mother in Old Marston Lane. It is not yet clear if and where the family came together again.

• Eliza Woolley, a widow aged 53, had married into one of the most extensive families of Tutbury glassworkers, and was living at 4 Second Avenue, Rushenden with her three Tutbury-born sons, Joseph aged 23, George aged 19 and Edward aged 13. Joseph was a Learman and George a Gatherer at the Bottle Works. There is some uncertainty about his age, but it appears that Edward was killed on 3rd July 1916 at the Battle of the Somme. George was married on the Isle of Sheppey later in 1911 to Daisy Walkman and their son George T Woolley was born there in 1915. George Woolley junior found his way back to Tutbury by 1937 where he married Marjorie Wardle and became one of the best-known local Cutters of the Webb Corbett era.

• Charles Bowley aged 51, born in Burton, was a Labourer at the Sheppey Glassworks in 1911. His Tutbury-born wife Sarah nee Bell (1860-1935), daughter of Benjamin Bell, and their daughter Mabel, were still in Tutbury, but later moved to Kent to join him. Charles and Sarah both died in Queenborough.

166

F. Corbett & Co Dovedale Outing Photo Identities 1910

Figure 47 - At the Peveril of the Peak

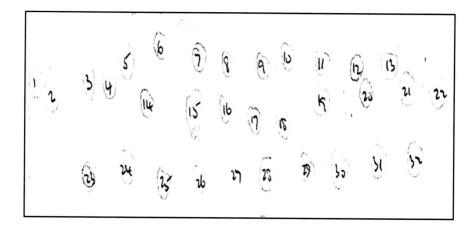

	Name	Age in 1911	Occupation
1	Samuel Sharp	29	Teazer
2	Harry McGuiness	44	Glass Blower
3	George Cresswell	51	Packer
4	Charles Marshall	35	Foreman Glass Cutter
5	James Cooke	53	Flint Glass Blower
6	Phillip McGuiness	39	Glass Blower
7	William Barker	58	Glass Cutter
8	?	-	-
9	Michael Molloy	57	Glass Blower
10	James Woolley	46	Flint Glass Maker
11	William Pavey	33	Flint Glass Blower
12	William Nicklin jun.	26	Glass Blower
13	James Corfield?	59	Glass Blower
14	Thomas Woolley	37	Glass Blower
15	William Blood	69	Joiner
16	Francis Crossley	44	Glass Etcher
17	Arthur Barker	20	Glass Cutter
18	Richard Irons	17	Glass Cutter
19	Joseph Siddalls	49	Glass Cutter
20	William Nicklin, sen.	46	Glass Maker
21	Frank Pegg	28	Engineer's Fitter
22	Thomas Attwood Corbett	37	Mould Maker
23	?	-	-
24	George Woolley	50	Glass Blower
25	John Orchard	57	Engraver
26	George Harry Corbett	54	Flint Glass Manufacturer
27	William Reynolds	32	Manager of Glass Works
28	Joseph Scotton	60	Glass Cutter

29	Samuel Siddalls	25	Clerk
30	George Compson	36	Glass Blower
31	? Stanley	-	-
32	John Lock	60	Glass Cutter

Figure 48 – Helpfully hatless
(and George Woolley still showing his best profile)

APPENDIX

G. Webb's Crystal Glass Employee Listing June 1921

Name	Age	Occupation	Residence	Birthplace
William Scriven	45	Bulb Blower	Bridge St, Tutbury	Tutbury
Frederick Kightly	33	Bulb Blower	Bridge St, Tutbury	Northampton
William Walker	13	Blower Attendant	Bridge St Tutbury	Tutbury
Fredrick Bradbeer	14	Machinist	Bridge St, Tutbury	Scropton
Frederick Hodson	19	Bulb Blower	Bridge St, Tutbury	Marston
William Naylor	46	Mould Dresser	Bridge St, Tutbury	Lancashire
James Gorton	25	Bulb Maker	Burton St, Tutbury	Tutbury
Percy Bowring	24	Bulb Blower	Burton St, Tutbury	Willington
Philip McGuiness	22	Labourer	Burton St, Tutbury	Tutbury
George Rumbelow	18	Bulb Packer	Burton St, Tutbury	Norfolk
Frances Bridges	21	Clay Worker	Castle St, Tutbury	Tutbury
Charles Shann	41	Manager	Castle St, Tutbury	Wolverhampton
George Cresswell	61	Bulb Packer	Castle St, Tutbury	France
May Parker	16	Bulb Wrapper	Church Lane, Tutbury	Tutbury
Gladys Young	20	Typist	Church Lane, Tutbury	Melbourne
Samuel Ward	30	Bulb Blower	Church Lane, Tutbury	Lichfield
Ernest Shilton	29	Labourer	Church Lane, Tutbury	Ashbourne
James Holden	49	Stoker	Church Lane, Tutbury	Littleover
Henry Ratcliffe	13	Machine Attendant	Cornmill Ln, Tutbury	Burton
Joseph Priestly	26	Gatherer	Cornmill Ln, Tutbury	Tutbury
Thomas Shilton	35	Teazer	Cornmill Ln, Tutbury	Tutbury
John Bentley	46	Bulb Blower	Cornmill Ln, Tutbury	Tutbury
James Harlow	50	Labourer	Duke Street, Tutbury	Tutbury
Harold Bradshaw	20	Labourer	Duke Street, Tutbury	Hilton
Edgar Gent	13	Bulb Blower	Duke Street, Tutbury	Tutbury
Harry McGuiness	23	Pot Maker	High Street, Tutbury	Tutbury
John Hill	42	Teazer	Ludgate St, Tutbury	Burton

Ernest Baines	23	Bulb Blower	Ludgate St, Tutbury	Newborough
William Pavey	43	Glass Maker	Ludgate St, Tutbury	Birmingham
John Keeling	65	Labourer	Ludgate St, Tutbury	Birmingham
Cyril Moore	14	Bulb Maker	Ludgate St, Tutbury	Tutbury
Alice Nicklin	18	Bulb Packer	Monk St, Tutbury	Tutbury
Thomas Moston	23	Labourer	Monk St, Tutbury	Tutbury
George Bennett	56	Labourer	Tutbury	Tutbury
Thomas Wood	15	Machine Attendant	Monk St, Tutbury	Hatton
Ruth Fearn	17	Bulb Wrapper	Monk St, Tutbury	Tutbury
William Press	21	Bulb Blower	Monk St, Tutbury	Tutbury
John Raines	25	Bulb Blower	Monk St, Tutbury	Newborough
George Woolley	29	Bulb Blower	Monk St, Tutbury	Tutbury
Evelyn Moorcroft	14	Bulb Packer	Monk St, Tutbury	Tutbury
Harold Bradshaw	15	Bulb Blower	Park Lane, Tutbury	Tutbury
Albert W Bennett	39	Blacksmith	Rolleston-on-Dove	Stretton
Albert F Bennett	14	Blower's Assistant	Rolleston-on-Dove	Scropton
Arthur Grimley	22	Glass Mixer	Rolleston-on-Dove	Rolleston
Harry Bentley	15	Glass Worker	Rolleston-on-Dove	Rolleston
George DeVille	19	Glass Maker	Scropton	Hatton
Thomas Smith	32	Stoker	Hatton	Burton
William Edwards	29	Bulb Blower	Hatton	Hatton
Ernest Hough	40	Glass Worker	Hatton	Foston
George Blood	16	Glass Gatherer	Hatton	Tutbury
Horace Bridges	16	Glass Worker	Hatton	Hatton
Albert Hodson	23	Bulb Blower	Hatton	Hatton
Ernest Shaw	13	Labourer	Hatton	Hatton
Wilfred Ward	14	Machine Attendant	Hatton	Hatton
George Blood	15	Machine Assistant	Hatton	Tutbury
Tom Brassington	15	Machine Assistant	Hatton	Draycott
Joseph Siddalls	59	Pot Maker	Hatton	Burton
Mildred Siddalls	18	Factory Hand	Hatton	Tutbury
Hilda Johnson	21	Bulb Wrapper	Hatton	Hatton

Harold Johnson	18	Bulb Blower	Hatton	Hatton
Charles Johnson	14	Blower's Assistant	Hatton	Hatton
Thomas Timmins	26	Bulb Blower	Hatton	Tutbury
William Nicklin	37	Bulb Maker	Hatton	Tutbury
Robert Nicklin	13	Bulb Apprentice	Hatton	Tutbury
William Gregson	14	Labourer	Hatton	Hatton
Lizzie Eaton	34	Forewoman	Hatton	Hatton
Wilfred Watson	18	Blacksmith	Hatton	Hatton
Jack Corden	18	Bulb Apprentice	Hatton	Scropton
Frank Pegg	38	Works Foreman	Hatton	Burton
William Adams	18	Bulb Blower	Hatton	Foston
Walter Duncan	49	Building Foreman	Hatton	Scotland
Albert Ridgard	36	Engine Attendant	Hatton	Winshill
Ada Nash	20	Bulb Examiner	Hatton	Hatton
George Bridges	40	Fireman	Hatton	Kirk Ireton
James Booker	23	Bulb Blower	Hatton	Derby
Charles Marshall	45	Bulb Examiner	Hatton	Tutbury
Jack Garland	20	Labourer	Hatton	Burton
Lillian Copestake	15	Bulb Packer	Hatton	Tutbury
Annie Coates	28	Bulb Sorter	Hatton	Lancashire
Gertrude Shaw	16	Bulb Examiner	Hatton	Burton

Notes:
"Bulb Blower" and "Bulb Maker" are interchangeable terms.
"Stoker", "Teazer" and "Fireman" also perform the same job of keeping the furnaces going.

172

APPENDIX

H. Trent Valley Glassworks Floods 1957-60

1. Flooding of Works - Tuesday 6th August 1957
Internal company report, 1957 (Museum reference GL 294)

"At approximately 11.45 a.m. on Tuesday 6th August 1957, the Works suffered serious flooding. The average depth of water throughout the works was 2 ft.

The flooding was not caused by the River Dove, but from surface water from an area south of Ashbourne. Apparently a very heavy storm occurred in the area of Snelston and Cubley during the night...when 5.2 inches of rain fell. This torrential rain caused extensive flooding of the Cubley and Foston Brook and also the Sutton Brook. This caused extensive damage to the bridge at Foston and other bridges in the area.

A flood warning was received at the Works at 10.30 a.m., when only a small maintenance staff were on duty as the Works were closed for the Annual Holiday. Immediate action was taken to remove motors from the Compressor House to a higher level and to sandbag up all the entrances to the main building.

...At about 11 a.m. some fields in the direction of Scropton were seen to be under water, and reports were received at the works that the floods were approaching rapidly. At approximately 11.15 a.m. the approach of the flood water could be heard and at approximately 11.20 a.m. the field opposite the factory was flooded and water soon came over Scropton Lane into the works. By this time a Fire Pump from Tutbury was in attendance and pumping from the basement of the Furnace commenced shortly after this, water having entered the main building very rapidly.

Previously, contact had been made with Mr Pritchard of Teisen to ascertain what action should be taken in the event of flooding, and in view of

173

information given, no firing had taken place since the flood warning was received. Arrangements were made to draw the fires in the event of serious flooding. It was obvious at this point that serious flooding would occur and this action was taken immediately.

However, the flood water entered the works at such a rate that within ten minutes of pumping commencing, the Tutbury Fire Pump was under water and out of action, and orders were given by the Fire Brigade to clear the building immediately in case of explosion. In consequence of the speed with which flooding took place, it was impossible to draw the fires on either furnace and by the time the main building was cleared, it was impossible to effect any salvage from any other part of the factory premises.

No explosion took place, but it was impossible to remain in the basement around the Furnaces owing to the fumes. A large quantity of steam was given off, and this continued for a considerable time. Owing to the depth of the water around the Furnaces, it was obvious at the time that there was no hope of saving these, and it was only possible to wait and see how quickly the water would go down.

The following are various depths of the flood: -
Mr Bennett's Office   25"
Fitters (By Shaper)   5"
Main Switch under Furnace by Stoppering Shop 39"
Decorators   28"
Box Store   36"
Compressor House   32" (by back wall)

On No.1 Furnace, the water reached the bottom of the second row of recuperator tubes from the top - a depth of approximately 68". On No.2 Furnace, the water reached the top of the second row of tubes from the top - a depth of 65". The level of the water only rose very slightly between 12 and 1 p.m., and then started to fall. By 7 p.m. on Tuesday 6th it had fallen approximately 1 ft. It was obvious on Tuesday evening, that nothing could be done until the water level dropped considerably, and a Teazer and one man were left as night watchmen during the night.

On the morning of Wednesday 7th, the water level had dropped considerably, and Scropton Lane was clear, but water still extended just beyond the Decorating Shop, and there was approximately one and a half feet of water in the factory yard. By this time a number of Fire Pumps were in attendance, and contact was made with Mr Cox who stated that there was no purpose in commencing pumping the works until the water level had dropped still further. He thought this would not be until the following day, Thursday.

The level continued to drop during the day and in view of the urgency of clearing water from the Furnaces, contact was made with Mr Cox later in the day, and he said that he would do his best to start pumping Wednesday evening if possible. Pumping did commence during later afternoon on Wednesday 7th.

Consideration was then given to the possibility of installing a Gas Pipe into the back of No.1 Furnace with a view to maintaining a temperature of at least 600 deg. centigrade which was the temperature at that time. The matter was discussed with Mr Pritchard, and he thought that it was worth trying. An approach was made to the East Midlands Gas Board, who came immediately to see what equipment was necessary. Installation of a 3" pipe commenced at 8 p.m., and was completed shortly before 12.30 a.m. on Thursday. In the meantime, Mr Gascoyne of the Gas Board fixed a limit on the gas available, and it was obvious that there would not be sufficient gas to consider trying to save both furnaces. It was decided to use the available gas on No. I. Furnace. Shortly before 1am., the Gas Pipe was in operation, and kept on until the fires had been brought into use.

As a result of this flooding, it is obvious that every possible effort must be made to keep all electric motors and electrical installations as high as possible. Although nothing at all could have been done to save the Furnaces in a flood of this nature, more powerful pumps would be invaluable if slight flooding were experienced.

It is also vital that both Furnaces should be equipped with the necessary installation to use Gas in the event of flooding. An approach must be made to the East Midlands Gas Board regarding an adequate supply. It is understood that a larger main is to be laid in Scropton Lane in the near future. If such a supply of gas were available on both Furnaces immediately flooding occurred, it might be possible to save at least both Furnace Pot Chambers and Pots. There would undoubtedly still be a risk of damage to the recuperators below water level.

Also every effort should be made to store Glasshouse Pots in a very high position, where they would be away from flood water. In the event of a flood warning being received in future, every effort should be made to remove all electric motors likely to be submerged and all office records removed to safety. Further, the electricity supply should be cut off at the mains if it becomes apparent that serious flooding is imminent."

2. General Report on the Flooding of the Works on Sunday 4th December 1960

Internal company report, reference WHB/MJB, 1960. (Museum reference GL 294)

"Following an extremely wet Summer and Autumn with the ground in a saturated condition, heavy rain fell all day on Saturday 3rd December followed by a bad storm during Saturday night. It was reported that one and a half inches fell during this period. This heavy rainfall led to serious flooding of Hatton and district. By about 10 a.m. on Sunday morning some of the fields between Hatton School and the Uttoxeter Road were flooded but the general position remained static for some time. Production was stopped at 12.15 a.m. as the Glass Makers wanted to get home to move furniture etc. At about 12 noon the position began to deteriorate and the river Dove was rising rapidly following the very heavy rain. Repton Rural District Council gave out a flood warning.

Immediate action was taken at the Works to raise above flood level all possible stocks of raw materials, pots, finished goods, packing materials, office equipment etc. A start was made to dismantle compressors, vacuum pumps, electric motors and move them high out of possible flooding. In spite of the obvious difficulty in obtaining a large amount of labour, a great deal of this work was completed before the Works was flooded at 5.45 p.m.

During the afternoon the level of the water in the field on the west side of the Works continued to rise and water was pouring in through the culvert. By about 4 p.m. the position appeared very serious. The Dove was still rising and reached up to the Railway embankment on our side. Staton's railway bridge was covered and the Hatton - Tutbury Road under about three feet of water by the Plaster Mill. In view of experience during the 1957 flood when one Fire Service pump was drowned, the Fire Service was not called. It was felt that it would be impossible to keep the flood water out of the Works.

At approximately 5.35 p.m. water started to flow over the main drive and it became clear that within a short time the whole Works would be flooded. In view of this the electricity supply was switched off at the mains. (Electricity supply in the Scropton Road area was off for a short period between 5.30 and 6 p.m. but was on at all other times). As soon as it was clear that the furnace flues would be flooded, fire-doors on both furnaces were opened and the pots on the top of the furnaces also opened to avoid risk of explosion and consequent damage to the furnaces. Within 10 - 15 minutes the whole area around the furnaces was flooded to a depth of 3 - 5 feet. The water level continued to rise till 9.15 p.m., and then commenced to drop slowly.

The following are various depths of water: -
Mr Bennett's Office 23". Fitters by Shaper 3". Main switch under furnace by Stoppering Shop 37". Decorators 26". Box Store 34". Compressor House 30" by back wall. On No.1 furnace water reached just below the second row of recuperator tubes from the top - a depth of approximately 66". On number 2 furnace it reached near the top of the second row of tubes from the top - a depth of 63". These levels are 2" below those of 1957.

As soon as the glass house was clear of smoke and fumes all pot fronts were well clayed up in order to keep maximum heat in the furnace and during the early part of the night a good gas supply was fed into the pot chambers for both Nos.1 and 2 furnaces, in order to maintain the temperature as far as possible.

177

The position at 9 a.m. on Monday December 5th was that the level of the Dove had dropped considerably and the water level in the Works had also gone down. The yard was still flooded to a position just beyond the Decorating shop and the level was half an inch below the step outside the General Office (now the Training Centre). Furnace temperatures were - No.1 1040°C and No.2 960°C. Mr Bailey telephoned to say that he had instructed the Fire Service to attend immediately with all available pumps and during the morning four were in attendance pumping from the yard into the field on the Scropton side of the Factory. By this time, the level of the Dove had dropped and water was flowing from this field back through the culvert into the river.

As the level of water in the yard had dropped it was decided to sand-bag up the main entrance to the furnaces by the Stoppering Shop and between the Compressor House and No. 2 furnace - also all possible inlets, and to pump from inside the building into the yard. This operation proved very successful and the water level around the furnaces dropped rapidly. A large pump from Fauld was used for this while the remaining pumps operated from sumps in the yard. As the water level dropped still further our small pumps were used to clear the firing-on ends of No.1 and 2 furnaces. By late Monday afternoon all except two pumps had been withdrawn.

By about 5 p.m. on Monday the No.1 furnace flues were clear of water and as fires were still going it was decided to continue firing-on. The temperature at this time was 880°C. The Fauld pump was withdrawn at 7 p.m. and a 350 - 500 Coventry Climax Fire Service Pump took over and continued to pump from the sump by No. 2 furnace flues. At this time the flues were still under water but the general water level was dropping.

At about 1 a.m. on Tuesday, No. 2 flues were partially clear of water and it was possible to start firing. The temperature at that time was 890°C. It was noted that once the furnace flues on No. 2 were partially clear of water, a reasonable chimney draft was obtained and there was little or no flame outside the pot chamber. However, on No.1 furnace nearly all the gas was burning outside and not inside the pot chamber. It was realized that on No.1 Furnace there was very little if any secondary air.

178

During Tuesday morning the temperature of No.2 furnace rose steadily but No.1 dropped until it was down to 810°C. The temperature of No.2 was then 1100°C.

During Tuesday morning it became clear that No.1 Furnace had suffered considerable damage to the recuperator tubes etc., and this was causing shortage of secondary air. As the temperature continued to drop all day it was decided that there was no hope whatever of saving No.1 furnace and that it would need a repair. During Tuesday evening and night the pot fronts were taken down and pots cleared so that Mr Pritchard of Teisen could inspect the furnace on Wednesday.

When the flooding occurred all pots on both furnaces were full and when those on No.2 furnace were inspected on Wednesday there appeared to be no damage to them. As the temperature of No.2 continued to rise it was decided on Wednesday evening that production could commence at 10 a.m. Thursday and plans were made accordingly."